Blackwell
**Modular
Science**
Key Stage **3**

Earth, Atmosphere and Space 1

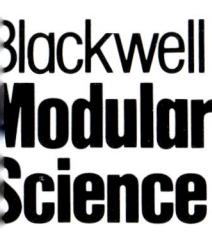

The Blackwell
Science
Programme
5-16

James Bradberry

© James Bradberry 1990
Design and illustration © Basil Blackwell Ltd

First published 1990
Published by
Basil Blackwell Limited
108 Cowley Road
Oxford OX4 1JF

Acknowledgements

The author and publishers would like to thank the following for permission to use photographs:

Allsport *17D*; Armagh Observatory *60A*; Patrick Bailey *57C, D* and *E*; Barnaby's *40A*; Biofotos *27D, 46B*; Blue Circle Cement *41D*; British Geological Survey *29E*; C S Broomfield *11B*; Cadbury External Services *22A*; European Space Research and Technology Centre *14B*; J F P Galvin *13C*; Geoscience Features *23E, 24B, 26C, 35B, 35D, 43B, 48A, 49E*; HMSO *14A, C* and *D*; John Highfield *16A*; Holt Studios *54A*; Eric Kay *22C, 28B, 28C, 44B, 46A, 53C*; Alfred McAlpine *41C*; David McConnell *11F*; Natural History Museum *22b, 23F, 23G, 30C, 35C, 38B, 42C*; Oxfam *18A*; Popperfoto *50A*; Wilhelm Schmid *11C*; Harry Smith *4A*; *Solo 36B*; Graham Topping *26A*; University Museum, Oxford *38A*; US Geological Survey *47D*; J A Walton *11D*; David A Warrilow *11E*.

British Library Cataloguing in Publication Data
Bradberry, James
Earth, atmosphere and space.
1. Earth sciences
I. Title
550

ISBN 0-631-90504-9

Produced by AMR
Typesetting by Microset Graphics Ltd, Basingstoke
Illustrations by Tek Art
Printed in Singapore by Kin Keong Printing Co Pte. Ltd

Key to icons used in text	
IT	
CA	computer application
CP	computer program
DTP	desk top publishing
SS	spreadsheet
WP	word processor
Safety	
👓	goggles
S	outdoor safety

PREFACE

This book is written to help you find out more about our fascinating planet, Earth. As you read it I hope you will want to find out more about it for yourself.

Just as detectives look for clues, so scientists look at evidence in the environment — the rocks, soil, rivers, beaches and sky, as well as other planets in the solar system — for clues about the importance of the natural processes that operate in our own world. The study of the Earth covers events that have happened over more than 4000 million years. During this time many forces have helped to make the Earth the planet it is today and many of these processes are still operating.

Finally, I wish to thank my family and everyone who has helped and advised me in the writing of this book. I hope you will enjoy working with the book as much as I have enjoyed writing it.

James Bradberry
Withywood School, Bristol

CONTENTS

WEATHER

1.1 The weather

What is weather?

The Earth is covered by a moving layer of air called the **atmosphere**. This layer is changing all the time. There are changes in how hot or cold the air is; how wet the air is; how fast the wind is (wind velocity); where the wind is blowing from (wind direction); how much rain; how much cloud and sunshine. All these changes make up the weather in a particular place.

'It's raining!' said Tom. 'I hate this bad weather.'

'You might think it's bad,' said Liz, 'but it's good for my garden!'

'But it's so cold,' said Lotti. 'If it was a bit colder it would be snowing and we could go sledging — that would be good.'

'You might think it would be good,' said Liz, 'but drivers hate snow — it makes the roads so slippery.'

Try this

Make a list of the people who would like or dislike the following kinds of weather:

Type of weather	Like	Dislike
rain
snow
wind
sunshine		

'Look at this report of a storm in the paper,' said Tom. 'I bet no one was glad about this happening. . .' But Tom was wrong – can you spot why?

16 October 1987

HURRICANE HITS SOUTH

LAST night southern Britain was hit by a big hurricane. 15 million trees were uprooted. 19 people were killed. Many houses and cars were damaged or destroyed. For most people it was impossible to travel anywhere and people found it difficult to get help by telephone. Many homes now have no electricity supply. There are a number of complaints that the storm was not forecast and that no warnings were given. Makers of quality furniture are expecting that supplies of oak will be easier to get hold of.

Activity 1.1

Can you help Tom answer these questions?

1 Make a list of at least five ways in which the storm had a big effect on people's lives.
2 What could have been the reason for people losing their electricity supply?
3 Give two reasons why it was difficult to travel anywhere.
4 If weather experts had warned of the storm, what precautions could people have taken?
5 All the words below are used to describe different kinds of storms. Copy them out, and write a sentence next to each one saying what it means. Use a dictionary to help you.

gale   hurricane
blizzard   tornado
thunderstorm   cyclone

A Storm damage, October 1987.

4

Activity 1.2

Measuring changes

It is possible to measure many of the changes in weather. Fig b is a graph of the number of hours of sunshine we had each day in the last week of May. Now answer the questions about it.

1 On which two days together did the sunshine equal that of Saturday?
2 On which day did it probably rain? Say why.
3 On which three days together did the sunshine equal that of Monday?
4 How many days had fewer than six hours of sunshine?
5 How many days had more than eight hours of sunshine?
6 How many hours of sunshine were there in the whole week?
7 Which day was the sunniest?

Activity 1.3

Recording what the weather is like

Using symbols is a useful, quick way of recording weather. Look at the example of the weather record for a week shown in Fig e. Fig c shows you what the symbols mean. Do you think the weather shown on the chart was recorded in spring, summer, autumn or winter? Say why.

Make your own weather recording chart for the next two weeks, using or adapting the symbols shown here. You could also record the amount of cloud cover using the cloud cover symbols suggested in Fig d. At the end of the fortnight look at your chart and answer these questions:

1 How many days were **a** sunny, **b** dry, **c** cloudy?
2 On how many days did it **a** rain, **b** snow, **c** hail, **d** thunder?
3 How many days were **a** cold, **b** warm, **c** hot?
4 How many days were windy?
5 Make scaled bar charts of your results, like the one shown in Fig b. **CP**

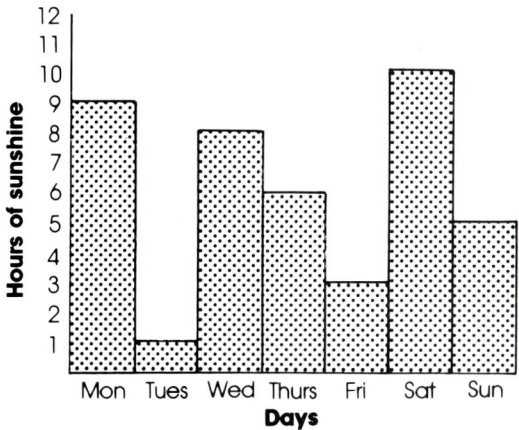

B

Weather	Symbol	Weather	Symbol
fog	F	sunny	
cold	C	sunny intervals	
warm	W	showers (rain)	
hot	H		
very windy		hail	
breeze		snow	
calm		thunderstorm	

Cloud amounts

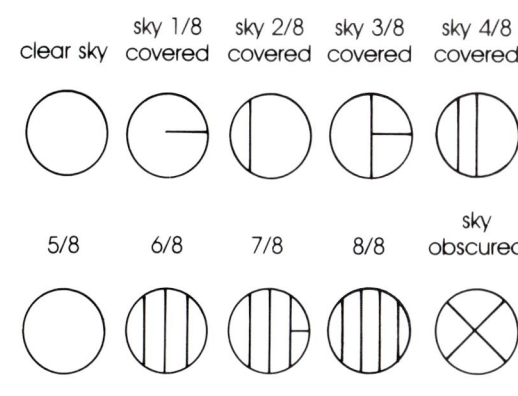

D Symbols for cloud cover.

Now try this

Compare your weather chart with one a friend has done, using the same symbols. Is it the same? Can you give reasons for any differences?

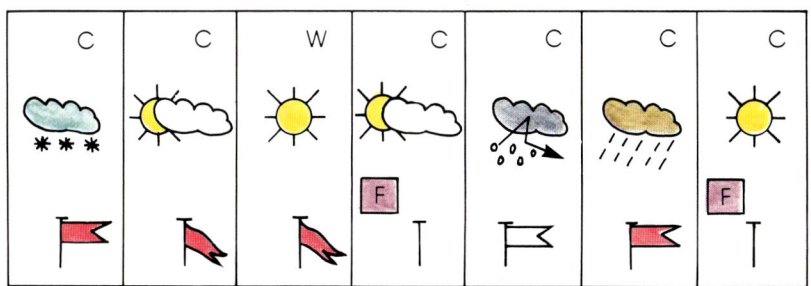

Monday   Tuesday   Wednesday   Thursday   Friday   Saturday   Sunday

E The weather record using symbols.

5

WEATHER

1.2 Symbols on maps

Symbols are often used on weather maps. You have probably seen them on the television and in newspapers. They are a quick way of telling people what the weather is like.

It was the day before Christmas Eve. Lotti, Liz and Tom were wrapping their Christmas presents. 'I hope the weather is nice today,' said Lotti. 'I've still got some cards to buy.' She picked up the newspaper to look at the weather maps. 'I don't understand this,' she said. 'What do these numbers and funny symbols mean?' The others were too busy to answer. Can you help explain to Lotti what they mean?

Activity 1.4

(WP) Decide what to write in a short report to Lotti about the maps shown in Fig a.

1 There are four different kinds of cloud symbol. In your report, draw each one and write down what it stands for.
2 What do the numbers inside black, arrowed circles stand for? Would you say that it will get more or less windy as the day goes on?
3 What do the numbers next to the cloud symbols stand for?
4 What do the wave symbols tell you?
5 Why are there two maps? What are the main differences between the two maps?
6 Can you tell Lotti what kind of weather to expect? For example, would it feel warm or cold for the time of year?
7 If Lotti lives in London, when would be the best time for her to go shopping?
8 If Lotti lives in South Wales, when would be the best time for her to go shopping?

Notice how numbers are used on the weather maps in Fig a. The numbers next to the 'cloud' symbols stand for degrees of temperature in a scale called **Celsius**. Temperature is a way of measuring how hot or cold it is, and a **thermometer** is the instrument used to do this.

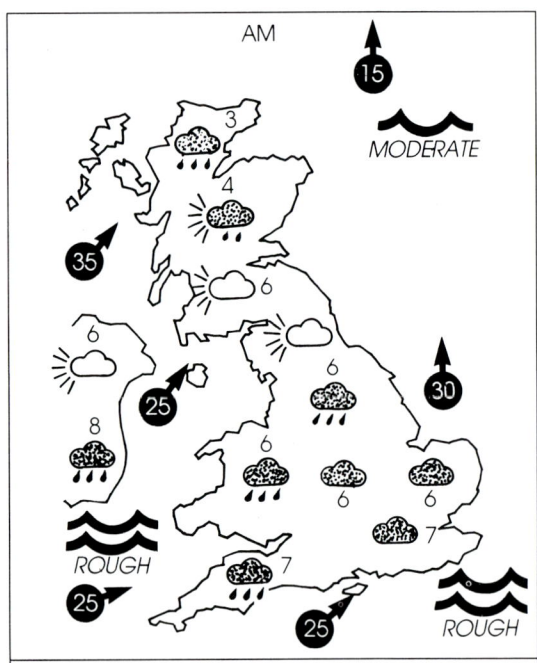

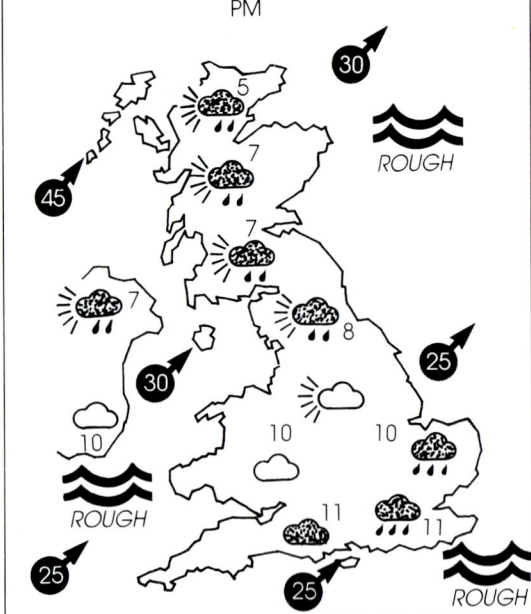

A Lotti's newspaper weather maps.

Activity 1.5

Measuring temperature (1)

Look carefully at a real example of a thermometer and compare it with Fig b. Make a sketch of the thermometer and label the **bulb**, the **capillary tube**, the **liquid** inside and the **scale** in degrees Celsius (°C). Find out if your thermometer contains mercury (silver colour) or alcohol (usually red).

1 Put your hand on the bulb. What happens to the level of the liquid in the tube? Can you explain why this happens?

2 What happens to the level if you take your hand away? Write down the final level of the liquid in degrees Celsius. This is your body temperature.

3 Find out if other people have the same body temperature reading.

4 Place the thermometer bulb in crushed ice in a beaker. Watch the liquid level — does it drop or rise? Why is this? Record the final level of the liquid.

5 Place the thermometer in hot water in a beaker — does the reading drop or rise? Why is this? Record the final level of the liquid.

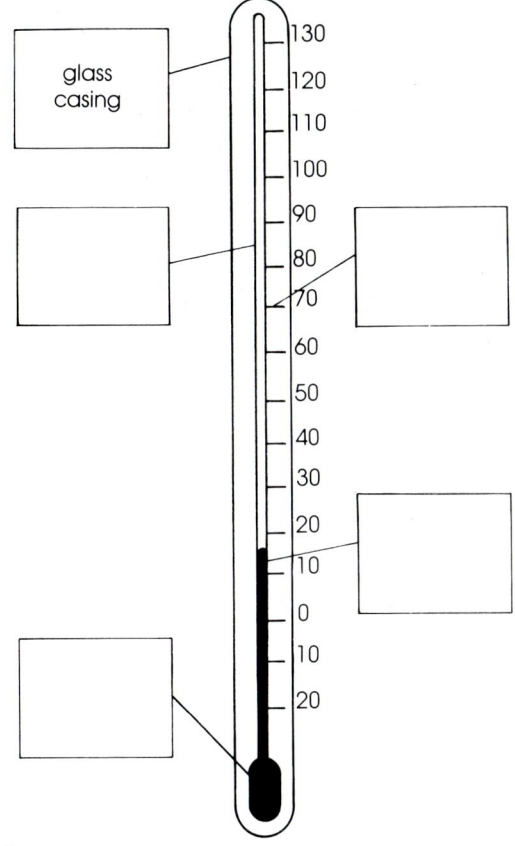

glass casing

B

Activity 1.6

Measuring temperature (2)

Now that you are familiar with how a thermometer works, you can use it to measure the temperature in different places both inside and outside the building. You could record the temperature on a table like this:

Place	Temperature (°C)
on my desk near the window near the radiator in sunshine (inside) outside in the sun outside in the shade a windy place a sheltered place	

Copy and complete these sentences, filling in the missing information.

1 The hottest place I found was _____ where I recorded the highest _____ of _____ degrees Celsius.

2 The coldest place I found was _____ where I recorded the _____ temperature of _____ degrees Celsius.

Now try these

Measuring air temperature over one week

(CP) Put the thermometer in a shady place outside and write down the temperature reading at the same time each day, eg in the lunch-hour. Record the temperature for a week. Make a bar chart of your results using graph paper.

Make your own weather map

Trace two map outlines from the weather maps in Fig a — for a.m. and p.m. Then use the symbols to record this weather:

A frosty start, with heavy showers spreading south along the eastern side of the country. There will be gales in the north, with blizzards in northern Scotland. In South Wales and Cornwall it will be a sunny day with broken cloud.

WEATHER

1.3 Estimating weather

Lotti, Liz and Tom were on holiday and they decided to go swimming. They began to argue about how warm the water was. Tom had just finished the washing up, so his hands were hot. Liz had just finished helping her mum de-ice the freezer, so her hands were cold. . .

When people talk about the weather, what they say often depends on how they are feeling. Opinion can vary a lot, especially when people are deciding how hot or cold it is. You can try this with your friends!

Activity 1.7

Estimating today's weather
Get each person in your group to choose one word or phrase from each of the lists below to describe today's weather. Then see how many of your friends use each word/phrase by drawing a bar chart to show their choices.

List 1	List 2	List 3
freezing cold	dry	calm
cold	damp	fresh
quite cold	quite wet	slight breeze
cool	wet	windy
warm	very wet	very windy
hot	muggy/humid	stormy

Do most people agree on the words they use to describe the weather? In which list did you find the greatest difference of opinion? You will realise by now that people don't always agree. One person might think it hot when another person thinks it is cold. A better way to record weather is to use instruments and measure it.

Measuring temperature
It is easy to measure temperature — how hot or cold it is — using a thermometer. Look at the diagram of a maximum/minimum thermometer (Fig b). This has a U-shaped tube, giving two sets of readings. This instrument allows you to record the highest (maximum) and lowest (minimum) temperature in 24 hours.

A Can you write the speech bubbles for Tom and Liz?

WP *Try this*

What do you think Tom said? What do you think Liz said? Match these up to the speech balloons in the cartoon.

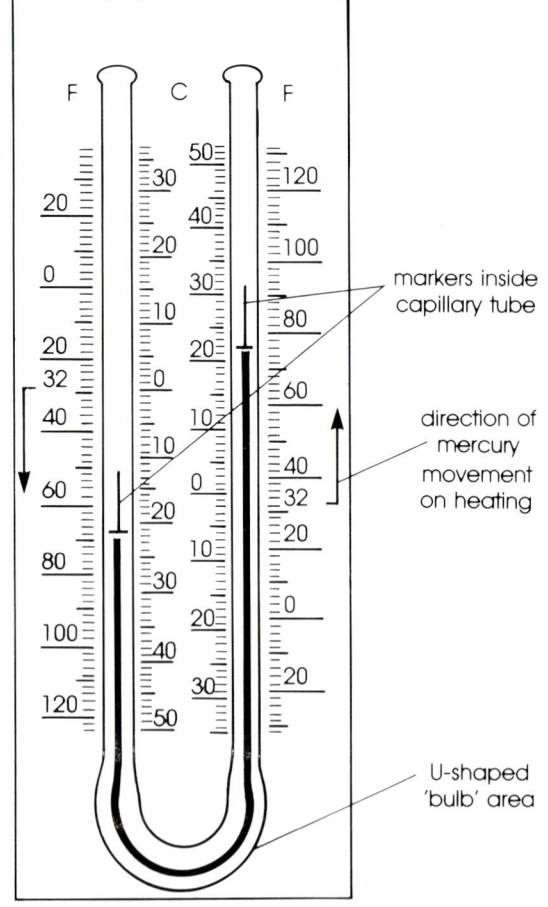

markers inside capillary tube

direction of mercury movement on heating

U-shaped 'bulb' area

B The maximum/minimum thermometer.

Activity 1.8

Before using the maximum/minimum thermometer you need to set the markers in the tube so that they are touching the liquid. To see how the mercury moves the markers, put your hands on the bulb area of the thermometer.

1 What happens to the markers?

Next place the thermometer in crushed ice.

2 What happens to the markers this time?

3 Can you still read what the higher temperature was?

4 Which end of the marker records the temperature?

5 Use this instrument to record the highest and lowest **(CP)** temperatures through the week. Don't forget to reset the markers each day. Make a line graph of your results on graph paper. It might look something like the graph shown in Fig c.

How much does it rain?

Tom found this project on the back of his magazine. He decided to try to find out for himself how much it rained. Can you help?

Activity 1.9

How much does it rain in my garden?

Before you can answer this question you need an instrument. The instrument used to measure rainfall is called a **rain gauge**. It is designed to funnel rain into a container. It is easy to make your own rain gauge:

Cut a 2-litre lemonade bottle about one-third of the way down using sharp scissors. Turn the top part upside-down to form a funnel. Push it into the bottom part of the bottle. Position your rain gauge partly buried in soil or weight it with pebbles. Put a collecting jam jar inside. It is best if the top of the gauge is about 20 cm above the ground. Keep a daily record by collecting the rainwater at the same time each day. Pour it into a measuring cylinder marked in millilitres (ml) and write down the amount and date on a chart. Your chart might look something like this:

Date	Amount in ml
23.10	5 ml
24.10	13 ml

When you have measured rainfall for a fortnight or so, make a bar chart of your results.

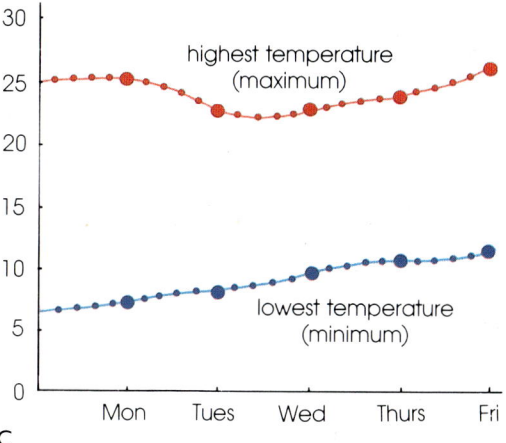

Temperature in degrees Celsius

highest temperature (maximum)

lowest temperature (minimum)

C

Activity 1.10

(WP) Comparing measurements of rainfall

If you and your friends all use the same size bottle, you could carry out a group investigation. Make sure you all take your readings at the same time each day for the same number of days. Here are some ideas that you could test: Does it rain more in my garden than in my friend's garden? Does it rain more in open spaces away from buildings? Is it true that less rain reaches the ground under trees? Does it rain more on higher ground? Is it true that weekends are the wettest two days of the week?

When you have some results, make daily bar charts of your figures. Then write about what you have found out.

Now try these

1 Why did Tom and Liz have such different feelings about the water temperature?

2 If you were using a maximum/minimum thermometer, when, in 24 hours, would you get the highest and lowest temperatures?

3 Write about some of the problems you came across in making and using the rain gauge.

WEATHER

1.4 Humidity and clouds

Water in the air

Lotti, Liz and Tom were about to spend their first day on holiday in a seaside chalet. 'The air smells musty,' said Lotti as they walked in.

'And this bed feels damp,' said Liz. 'Do you think the roof is leaking?'

'No,' said Tom. 'It just needs some fresh air. You two open the windows and I'll put the bedclothes in the airing cupboard.' What the children had discovered is that even if it is not raining, the air holds water. This is why clothes feel damp in cold rooms and beds need airing if they have not been slept in for a long time. The amount of moisture in the air is called **humidity**.

How do clouds form?

Clouds are made of millions of tiny water droplets or ice crystals. They form because as air rises it expands and cools. Cool air will not hold as much water vapour as warm air, and the moisture forms water droplets or ice crystals.

Clouds and weather

Can different cloud types be a good guide to the weather? Yes, they can. White, feathery-looking, layered clouds usually mean the atmosphere is calm and settled. Black, towering, bubbly-looking clouds show that the atmosphere is disturbed and that rain is more likely.

Activity 1.11

How moist is the air?
Soak some white blotting paper in a solution of two parts cobalt chloride to one part salt. Allow the paper to dry out, then cut the blotting paper into cloud shapes and stick your 'clouds' onto a sky picture. Write down any colour changes you see in your 'clouds' over several days.
1 What colour do the 'clouds' go when the air is damp?
2 What colour do the 'clouds' go when the air is dry?

Activity 1.12

Making clouds in a bottle
Place about 3 ml of water in a large glass bottle (see Fig a). Then shake the bottle to wet the sides. Puff a little smoke into the bottle. This will help to form the 'cloud'. Then connect the bottle to a bicycle pump with rubber tubing. Pump air in until the cork suddenly blows out.
1 What has happened inside the bottle?
2 Try to explain why this happened. It may help you to know that when air suddenly expands, it cools.
3 What would have been happening to the air temperature as air was being pumped in?

The point of this activity is to show that clouds form as air expands and cools. Warm air rising above the Earth also expands and cools. As it does so, water vapour condenses to form clouds.

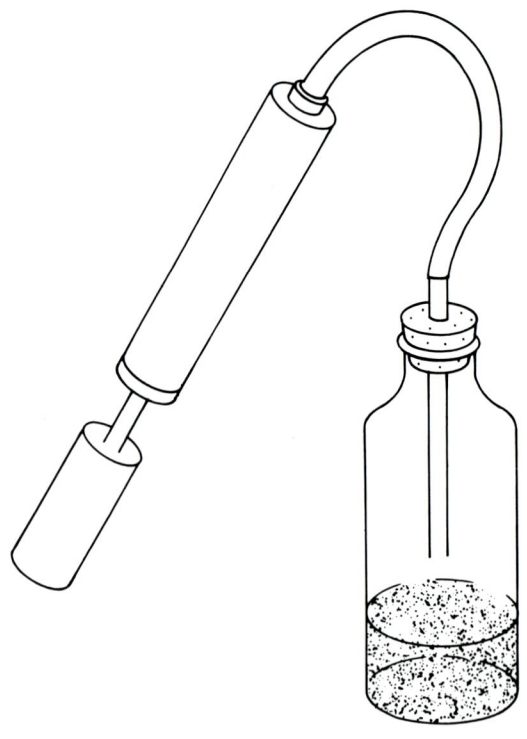

A What happens when air pressure suddenly forces the cork out?

B Alto-cumulus.

C Cumulo-nimbus.

D Cirrus.

E Nimbo-stratus.

F Cirro-cumulus ('mackeral sky').

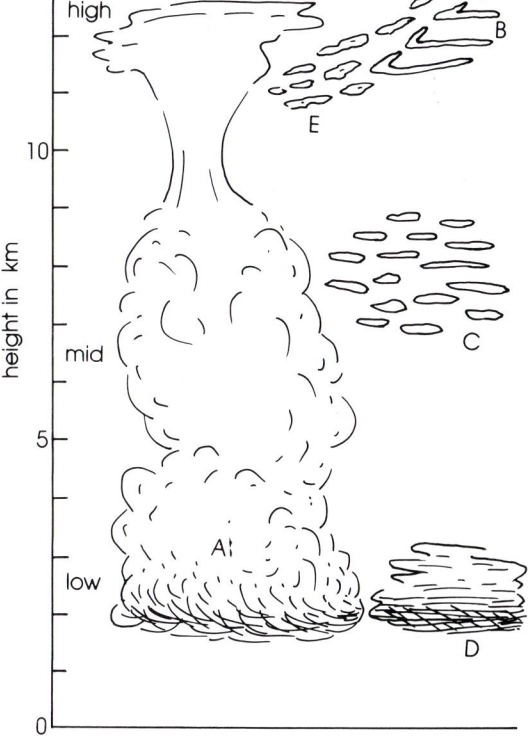

G Cloud heights.

Activity 1.13

Cloud types

Match up the five photographs (Figs b to f) — cirrus; cirro-cumulus; cumulo-nimbus, alto-cumulus, nimbo-stratus — with the descriptions **a** to **e** below. Look at the diagram of cloud heights (Fig g) as well.

a A fast-growing, bubbly cloud — dark at the base, towering from low to high level.

b A low-level layered cloud — often making it overcast, dull and wet.

c A high-level cloud — white, thin and feather-like.

d A mid-level cloud — puffy, whitish-grey, almond shape — in lines or rows.

e A high-level cloud — thin sheet or patch of cloud forming ripples or small, rounded masses — sometimes called a 'mackerel' sky because of the patterned appearance.

1 Which clouds do you think would be most likely to produce rain?

2 Which clouds do you think would be least likely to produce rain?

3 Look at Fig g and the descriptions **a** to **e**. Name the cloud types shown in the diagram. (1-5)

4 Write the height of the top and base of each cloud in the diagram.

Now try these

1 Select the most accurate word or phrase in the brackets to complete each of these statements:

a The gas that makes air is called (nitrogen/water vapour/steam).

b When it is raining, the air has 100 per cent (wetness/saturation/humidity).

c Air cools as it rises because it (expands/soaks up water/contracts).

d Cool air will not hold as much (moisture/cloud/humidity) as warm air.

2 Is it true that it is possible to forecast the weather from a study of cloud types? Find out more about cloud types from your local library. Then keep a record of the clouds you see each day, and the weather you experience. Is there any pattern?

WEATHER

1.5 Wind

Wind is an important part of our weather.

Try this

Which people in this list do you think would be most affected by the wind? postmen; drivers of high-sided vehicles; yacht sailors; aircraft pilots; people carrying open umbrellas; air balloonists; hang gliders.

It was a windy day so Lotti, Liz and Tom decided to go and fly their kites. They were having trouble getting the kites airborne. Lotti said, 'We need to work out exactly what direction the wind is blowing in.'

'That's a good idea,' said Liz. 'Then we can face the kites into the wind.'

Tom had a pocket compass with him. First he held up a handkerchief to see which way the cloth blew. 'Well, that's north over there, so. . . the wind is coming from the south-west,' he announced.

'So what?' said Lotti. 'Never mind all this north/south stuff — let's fly our kites!'

Tom had discovered that it was possible to measure wind direction in quite a simple way. Have you ever noticed windsocks at airports or weather vanes on church steeples? They are doing the same thing as Tom with his handkerchief. The direction the wind blows from is often linked with the kind of weather we have.

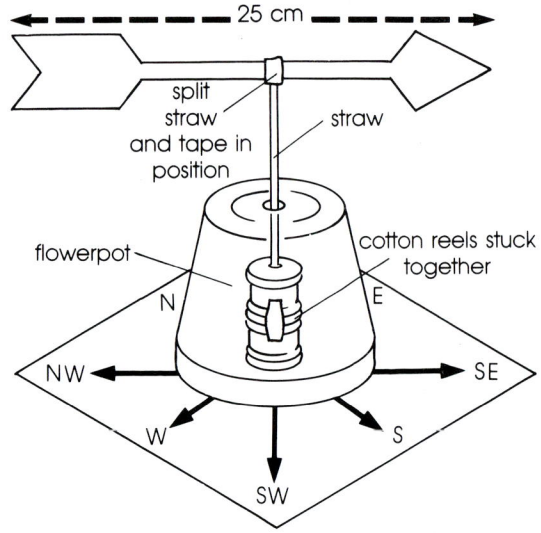

A A wind vane.

Activity 1.15

Measuring wind direction

Wind direction is measured using a **wind vane**. To make a wind vane you need a plastic straw, two large cotton reels, a small earthenware flowerpot and a piece of card.

Draw an arrow about 25 cm long on the card and cut out the shape (see Fig a). Then paint or varnish the card to waterproof it. Allow it to dry. Split the end of the straw and fit the card arrow into the slot, so that it balances. Then stick the straw and card together using parcel tape. Put the straw in the pot and cotton reels, as shown in the diagram. Mark out the compass directions using white paint on a piece of hardboard placed beneath the flowerpot.

Activity 1.14

WP Can you match up the following wind directions with the jumbled statements about the usual weather they bring to the British Isles in winter?

Wind direction	Usual weather
a northerly wind	warm and wet
an easterly wind	very cold, snow showers
a southern wind	
a north-west wind	biting cold weather, snow in north
a south-west wind	very warm, usually dry
	cool and wet

Write down what the usual weather would be in summer for each of these wind directions.

Activity 1.16

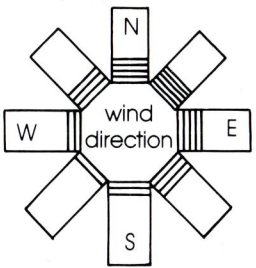

B A wind rose.

Estimating wind velocity (how fast the wind is)

One way to find out the velocity of the wind is to watch the effects of wind blowing on trees, leaves, smoke, drying clothes, kites, etc.

Activity 1.17

(WP) Make your own copy of this table. Then match the wind effects below to the wind descriptions.

Description of wind	Effects of wind
calm slight breeze moderate breeze strong breeze gale storm	

Effects of wind: whole trees sway; trees uprooted/damage to buildings; slight drift of smoke; tiles off buildings/difficult to walk; smoke rises straight up; small branches move/leaves rustle.

Measuring wind velocity

Wind velocity is recorded using an instrument called an **anemometer** (see Fig c). As the cups spin in the wind, the speed of the wind is recorded in miles or kilometres per hour.

Look again at the list of people affected by the wind at the start of this unit. Who in the list do you think would be most affected by high wind velocity? Who would be most affected by low wind velocity?

On the Severn road bridge near Bristol, there are anemometers. The bridge is often affected by high winds. At such times the owners will close the bridge to high-sided vehicles or restrict traffic to one lane only. Sometimes it has been closed altogether. Then the drivers have to go an extra 80 miles to cross the Severn Estuary.

Now try these

1 Copy the map outline (Fig d) and mark in the wind directions listed in Activity 1.14.
2 Write a short story or play (WP) about a lorry driver arriving at a bridge, only to be told the bridge had just been closed. Your group could then act out your play to the rest of the class.

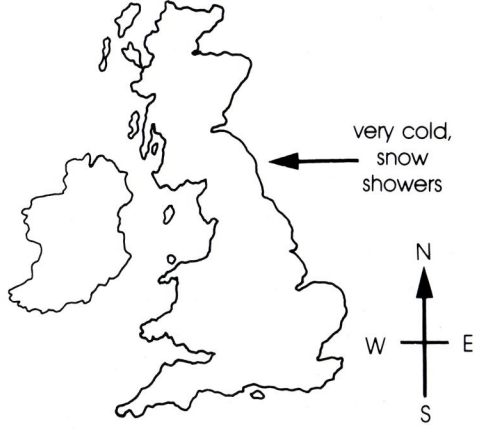

very cold, snow showers

D

WEATHER

1.6 Watching and forecasting weather

Daily weather forecasts are on radio, TV, in newspapers and even on the telephone. Where do they come from? Who puts them together? Who finds it all out?

Lotti, Liz and Tom were watching TV. Michael Fish was standing in front of his map again! 'How does he know all that?' said Liz.

'Beats me,' said Tom. 'Anyway, he's usually wrong.'

'I don't think he is,' said Lotti. 'I was reading that it takes hours of work to collect all the information. Look at what it says here. . .' Do you agree with Tom or with Lotti?

How the forecasts are made

First of all, there are over 7000 weather stations all over the world collecting and recording information about changes in the atmosphere. All large aircraft carry ASDAR (Aircraft to Satellite Data Relay). They measure wind speed and direction and temperature. All this is transmitted back to the ground via satellites. Even in remote places like deserts or the North Pole, unmanned automatic weather stations (AWS) record temperature, wind, air moisture and air pressure. They beam the data to manned weather stations using satellite links.

Weather balloons fitted with transmitters measure what it is like high in the atmosphere. The cloud patterns of different weather systems can be photographed from satellites like the one shown in Fig b and approaching storms can be seen easily. Rainfall patterns can be 'seen' on radar screens and a computer map can be made (see Figs d and e).

The main weather centre in Britain is the Meteorological Office at Bracknell. Here the computers process all the information coming in by satellite from all over the world. Twice a day a forecast of the world's weather is produced. Forecasters like Michael Fish have to look at this information and decide what they think will happen in the British Isles. Weather forecasts are provided for local areas through the telephone services like Weathercall (Fig c). Many people will pay for detailed forecasts. For example, a farmer is planning to spray his crops with insect poison. The only problem is that his field is next to a village, and he wants to be sure that the wind is blowing away from the houses. A fisherman wants to know if it would be safer to stay in harbour tonight.

A Michael Fish with the TV weather map.

B Satellites orbit the Earth at a height of over 1000 km.

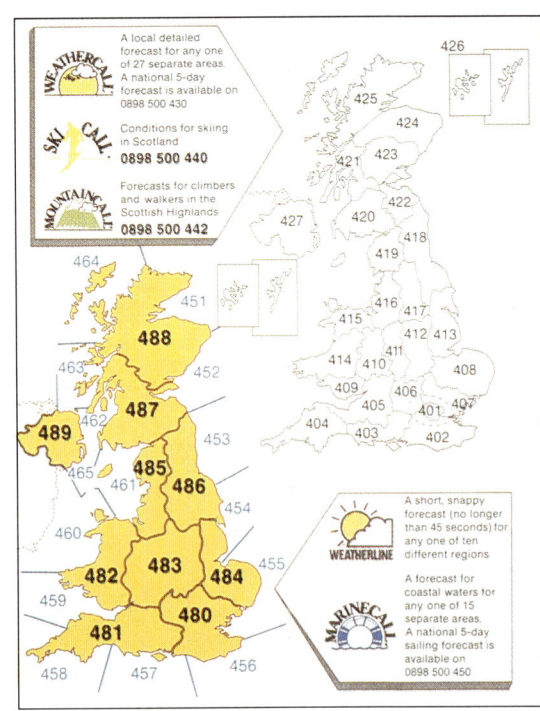

C Weather — a phone call away.

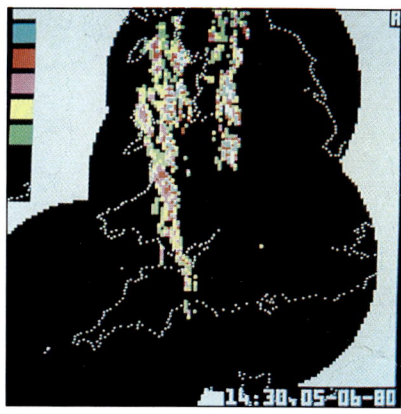
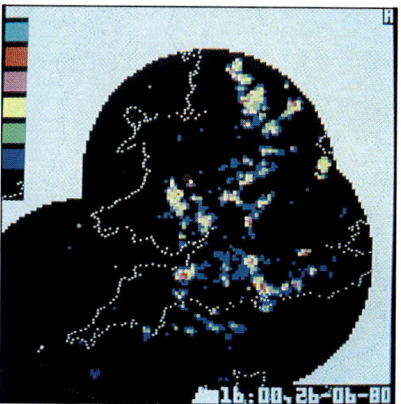

D A moving band of showers, detected by radar.

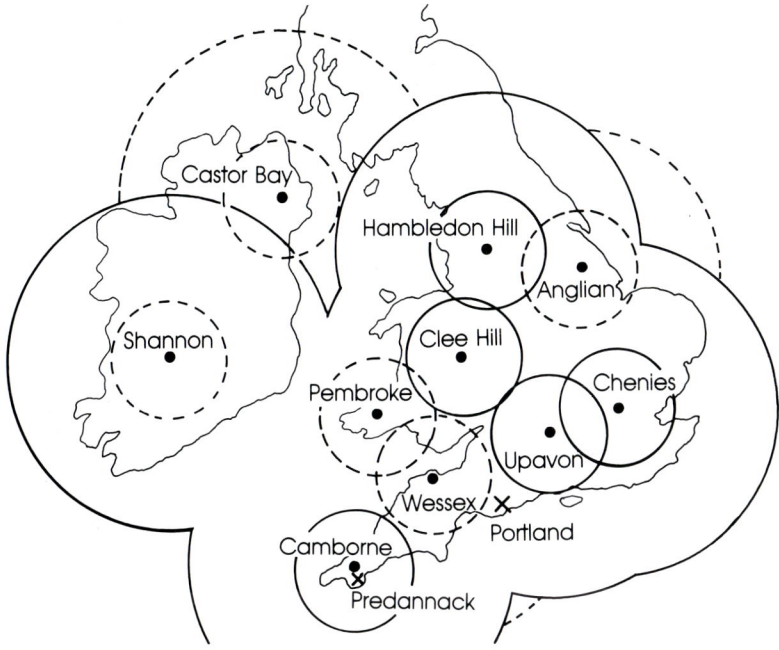

E Network of radar stations.

So how accurate are the forecasts?

Modern methods have greatly improved the accuracy of weather forecasts. For 24-hour forecasts, only about one forecast in every ten is wrong. For forecasts over five days ahead, three forecasts in every ten are wrong.

Activity 1.18

Cut out the weather maps from your daily newspaper for a fortnight. Then make your own 'silent weather movie' by sticking the maps onto pages of an exercise book. When you flick through you will see the weather change. Next to each map write down the date and what the weather was really like.

1 How many of the forecasts were correct?
2 Over the same fortnight, how many of the TV forecasts were correct?

Now try these

1 How many weather stations are there around the world?
2 Make a list of the different types of weather equipment mentioned in this unit.
3 Explain why satellites are so important in modern weather forecasting.
4 What technique is used to detect rain showers as they are happening?
5 You are a holidaymaker in North Wales. What number would you ring on Weathercall to hear a forecast?
6 It is February and you are a sheep farmer in Cumbria. You are worried about the ewes having lambs. Will it snow tomorrow? What number would you ring to find out?
7 How often are the forecasts updated on Weathercall?
8 Who supplies the information to Weathercall?
9 Is there ever a time when Weathercall is not available?

Possible homework

With your parents' permission, ring the Weathercall number for your area.

1 Make a note of the following: the forecast temperature, pressure and percentage humidity.
2 How many days ahead was the 'outlook'?
3 Write a short report on **WP** tomorrow's weather from what you have heard.
4 Trace or copy the outline of Britain from Fig c. Then, using your own symbols, make up a weather map to show tomorrow's weather.

15

WEATHER

1.7 How weather affects people

Lightning

Did you know that lightning is a huge electric spark? Did you know that, on average, five people are killed each year by lightning in England and Wales?

Lotti, Liz and Tom decided to go to the park to play. Just as they got to the park, there was a flash of lightning and a loud rumble of thunder. Then it started to rain heavily. 'Quick!' said Tom. 'Let's shelter under that oak tree!'

'No, we mustn't,' said Lotti. 'You can be struck by lightning if you shelter under trees.'

'That's just a fairy story,' sneered Tom. 'You get wet if you want to.'

'There are lots of other places to shelter,' said Lotti.

What is lightning?

Lightning comes from the build-up of electric charge on a cloud during a thunderstorm (Fig a). A lightning flash gets rid of a build-up of charge between the cloud and the ground, or between one cloud and another.

A The power of lightning.

Activity 1.19

Making lightning
Press Plasticine onto the middle of a baking tray. Then rub the tray round and round on top of a plastic bag (Fig b). Then pick up the tray by the Plasticine and hold something made of metal close to the corner of the tin. What do you see? Can you feel a tingling sensation?
Why it works: When the tray is rubbed on the plastic an electric charge builds up. This is called **static** electricity. It is the same kind of electricity that builds up in a thundercloud.

Activity 1.20

Magic combs
If your hair and comb are clean and dry, you could try these magic comb tricks. They all involve static electricity. Charge a comb by combing your hair hard (Fig c). Then try:
1 holding the comb above your head
2 holding the comb next to a trickle of tap water
3 holding the comb above small pieces of tissue paper.
In each case, watch what happens.

B

C

What lightning can do

People can be either hit directly by lightning and killed or seriously injured, or killed because lightning hits a tree or other object near to them. Lightning kills because it is a high voltage electric current.

Where are you most at risk?

It is dangerous to shelter under trees, but golfers sometimes get hit because they are out in the open (Fig d). In fact it is better to get wet because there is less risk of being hurt — if you are struck, the current will pass over you rather than through you. People holding metal objects are taking a risk. Metal builds up an electric charge, even if it has not been struck by lightning. Metal chains, medallions and other jewellery could cause a burn.

Activity 1.21

CP **Who is most at risk?**

Sort out this list under these headings: 'People most at risk', 'People least at risk'.

teacher; fisherman; golfer; windsurfer; office worker; farmer; housewife; fell walker; swimmer; gardener; bus driver.

Try to list them in order of risk. Who is most at risk?

Now try these

1 Where should the children have sheltered? What would have been the safest thing for them to do?

2 Look at the graph in Fig e.
   a Since 1850, which have been the three worst years for deaths from lightning?
   b Write down three examples of years with a low number of deaths.
   c Although the graph has its 'ups' and 'downs', what would you say is the general trend? Are there more or fewer deaths from lightning? Try to think of possible reasons for this.

3 Complete the lightning flash (Fig f) using these clues:
   1 The noise that lightning makes.
   2 The power in lightning.
   3 The start of it all.
   4 Lightning causes a lot of this.
   5 What you see when the discharge happens.
   6 It is probably safest in these.
   7 What you get if you are hit.
   8 Lightning will do this to five people each year in England and Wales.

D A safe, peaceful sport?

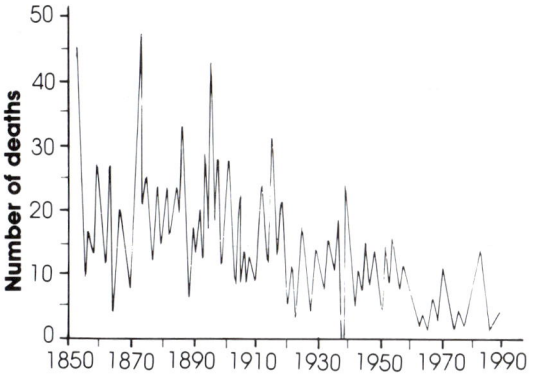

E Deaths from lightning in England and Wales.

F

WEATHER

1.8 When the weather turns nasty

Can you imagine 30 million people suddenly made homeless? Can you imagine a country the size of England with nearly all its bridges, roads and railways destroyed? But this did happen to Bangladesh. You might think a disaster like this would be caused by a war or a nuclear explosion — but you would be wrong. It's just because of the weather.

Liz and Lotti were worried. Their friend Tom had gone with his dad to Bangladesh to help with the disaster. This is why they were worried:

A Flooding in Bangladesh.

Flooding in Bangladesh threatens millions

Dhaka, 1 December 1988

MILLIONS of people struggled yesterday as the two great rivers — the Ganges and the Brahmaputra — overflowed their banks. The survivors are to be seen everywhere, clinging to tree trunks or living on the roofs of their houses. At least 3000 people are known to be dead so far. Many more are expected to die of disease and hunger in the next few days. A local reporter described the scene. . . 'I saw at least 300 bodies littered along the road. Survivors wander around crying for their mothers, fathers, brothers and sisters. They are burying 50 bodies in each grave'.

What is causing the flooding?

Bangladesh is often flooded because it is a low-lying delta where two rivers meet and flow into the sea over flat plains (see Fig b). The reason the country exists at all is because of the millions of tonnes of sand and mud brought down from the mountains by the rivers (see Fig c). Almost all the country is less than 15 metres above sea level. In 1988, heavy rains in the Himalayan mountains swelled the rising flood waters. The rivers overflowed their banks and over two-thirds of the country went under water. 110 million people struggled to survive.

How can the floods be controlled?

The slopes of the mountains used to be thickly forested. The trees used to 'soak up' the rain and their roots kept the soil in place. Recently they have been chopped down, so now the rainwater cascades straight down the slope. Much of the soil is washed away. The rise in flood water is much more sudden now because of this. (See Fig d.)

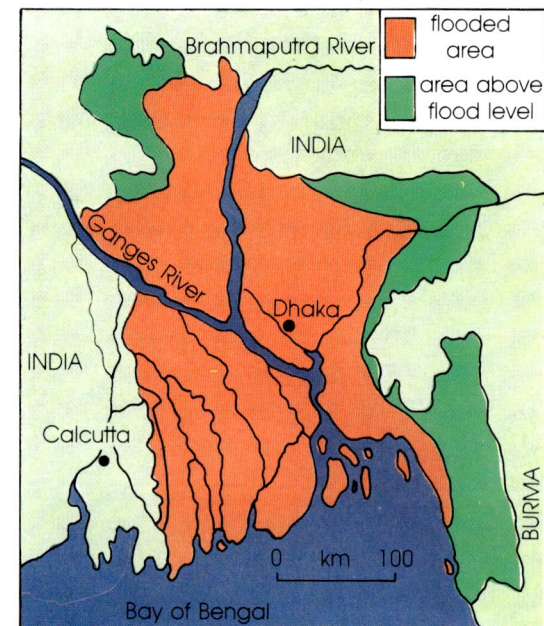
B Map of Bangladesh.

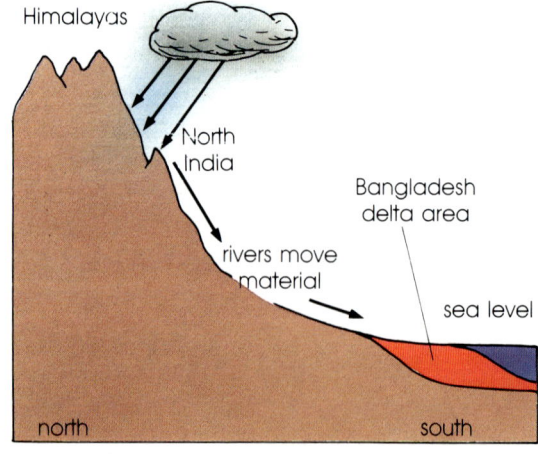
C Why there is a Bangladesh.

Activity 1.22

Here is a letter that Lotti has just received:

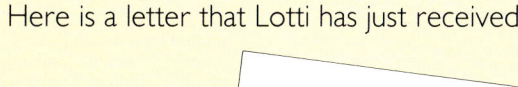

Dhaka
Bangladesh
31. 11. 88

Dear Lotti and Liz

At last I've found time to write to you.
It's terrible here. I've hardly seen Dad -
he's out all day with OXFAM trying to
help the people. There's no electricity, no
pure water, no food in the shops, and no
phones. But there's one good thing - the
school is flooded! We've heard another
storm is on its way. Write to me when
you can! I need cheering up. It's so
depressing here.

Best wishes
Tom

(WP) Write a reply to Tom and tell him what is being reported in this country.

Activity 1.23

How water runs off a slope

1 Make a slope of dry sand in a sand tray (Fig e).
2 Pour in a litre of water using a watering can fitted with a 'rose'.
3 How much run-off is there and what happens to the sand?

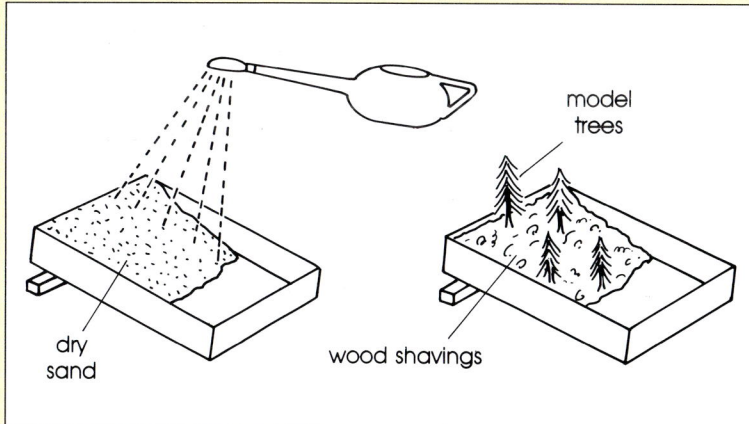

model trees

dry sand

wood shavings

E

4 Do the experiment again but add wood shavings to the dry sand, to bind together the surface like tree roots would do. You could even make some 'model' trees using nylon-wire brushes.
5 Pour on a litre of water. To what extent does the 'model forest' and its 'roots' prevent run-off?

impact of rain is absorbed by trees

water trickles into the river

roots of trees bind the soil together

river

Slow run-off (= less risk floods)

more erosion

water rushes in a cascade into river

soil thinner, because easily washed away

muddy river

Fast run-off (= floods)

D Do trees prevent run-off and erosion?

Activity 1.24

What can be done about it?

One suggestion for stopping the flood waters is to build dams across the rivers to hold back the water. Look carefully at Fig d. What else could be done to stop this kind of disaster happening again?

Now try these

1 How were so many people made homeless in Bangladesh?
2 How much of the country was flooded?
3 What is meant by a delta?
4 What happened in the Himalayas to cause the flood?
5 Produce a newspaper page **(DTP)** with headlines and stories, adding your group's suggestions for preventing future floods.

WEATHER

1.9 Water movements

What happens to the moisture in wet clothes as they dry? Why do the insides of windows mist up on cold days?

It was a showery day, but the children decided to go on a picnic by the river. It began to rain and they sheltered under a bridge, watching the river swirling past. By the time the children got home, the sun was shining again. Lotti noticed that the clothes were still on the washing line. 'That's strange,' said Lotti. 'Although it has rained, these clothes are nearly dry.'

'So what!' said Tom. 'I'm thirsty.' He went inside and brought them out a cola drink each.

'Hey! That's strange!' said Liz. 'Our cans are all wet on the outside.'

'That's because they are cold, silly!' said Lotti.

Tom sighed. 'I might as well do my homework. You two can help.' This is the page from Tom's book:

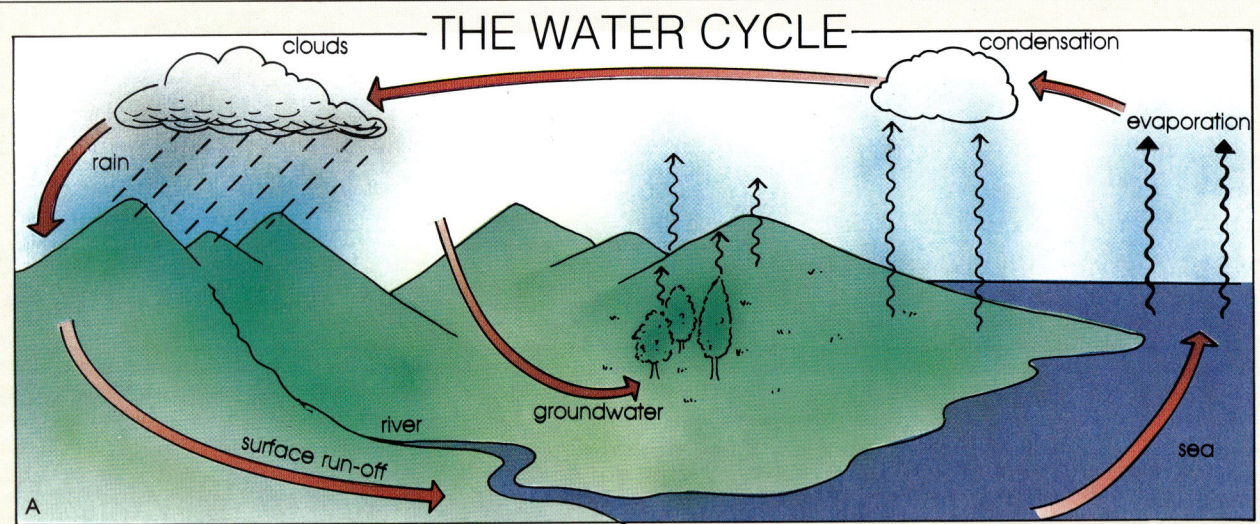

THE WATER CYCLE

clouds · condensation · evaporation · rain · groundwater · river · surface run-off · sea

Did you know that our planet has 1360 million cubic kilometres of water? Nearly all of this water is in the oceans.

The Sun's heat causes warmth and movement of air near the surface of the oceans – this makes some of the water change into the gas water vapour. This is called **evaporation**. As the water vapour rises into the air, it cools – tiny water droplets collect together to form clouds. This is called **condensation**. If this happens near the ground it is called mist or fog. The tiny droplets within the cloud unite to form bigger raindrops. Rivers carry rainwater to the sea, where it may evaporate again. This completes a circular movement of water, known as the **water cycle**. Some rain will soak into the soil to become groundwater. Plant roots pick up some of this moisture and release it back to the air through their leaves.

Homework Question: Explain what happens in the water cycle, giving everyday examples from your own experience.

Activity 1.25

1 What examples from the children's day could they give to explain the water cycle? Fig b may help you.
2 What part of the water cycle is shown by clothes on the washing line?
3 What part of the water cycle is shown by moisture on the cans of cola?

Activity 1.26

What is evaporation?

First find the mass of a damp towel. Then hang it out to dry, or dry it over a radiator. When it is dry weigh it again.
1 What is the difference in mass?
2 Why has the towel lost mass?
3 What is the mass of the water lost by evaporation?
4 Where has the water gone?
5 From what you have learnt in this activity, can you explain why clothes dry best on warm, sunny days?

Activity 1.27

Finding out about condensation

Compare a can of cola that has been in the fridge for a day with a can that has been at normal room temperature. Watch both cans. Which can becomes wet? Can you explain this? Where does the moisture come from?
Suspend the cold can above a dish, and blow cold air from a hair-dryer over a dish of water towards the can (Fig c). Note what happens. Repeat the procedure, this time blowing hot air. Does this make any difference?
1 Which method produced the most condensation on the can — blowing cold air over water, or blowing hot air over water?
2 What do these results tell you about the way water evaporates and condenses?
3 What did you see to show you that there is a water cycle? Make a sketch of the diagram and on your copy label 'evaporation', 'condensation' and 'rain'.

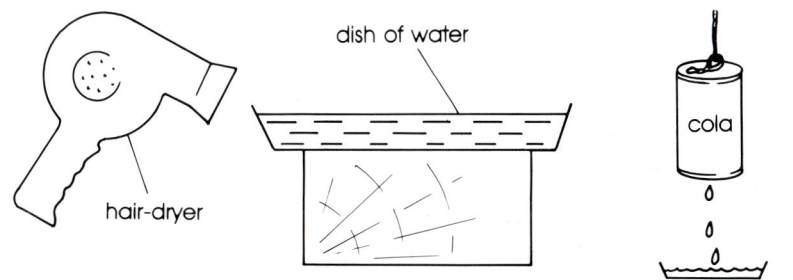

C Hair-dryer blows hot/cold air.

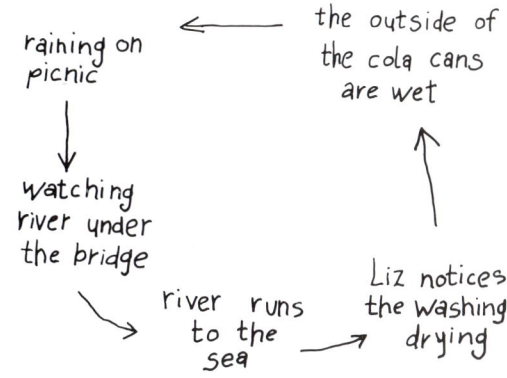

B Lotti's diagram.

Now try these

1 Write down the sentences that say what is happening most accurately:
   Evaporation: Clothes dry best when it is
   a warm, dry and breezy
   b warm but still.
   Condensation: Clouds form because
   a dry air rises and gets warmer
   b moist air rises and cools.
   Rain: This will only happen if
   a a cloud is at the right temperature
   b water droplets become heavy enough to fall.
2 Copy this diagram of the water cycle and fill in the missing words.

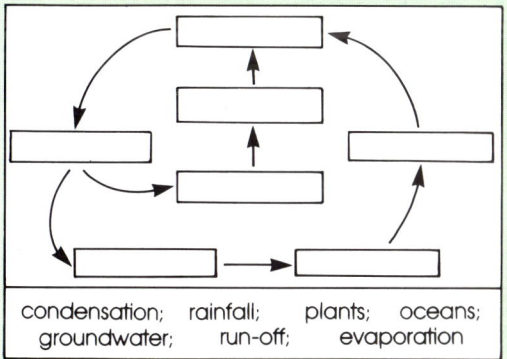

condensation; rainfall; plants; oceans; groundwater; run-off; evaporation

3 Make a list of everyday examples of parts of the water cycle you have seen, eg classroom windows misting up; running water in a kerb-side gutter; drying hair. Then draw a large diagram of the water cycle and write in your examples.

21

UNIT 2

ROCKS AND WEATHERING

2.1 Finding out about rocks

Lotti, Liz and Tom visited a sweet factory to see Crunchie bars being made. They watched the sugar, milk and syrup being mixed and heated in a big pan. As the hot mixture flowed out of the pan, air was injected into it under pressure. This made the mixture all bubbly and frothy. Then it was poured into moulds to cool and harden.

Liz picked up a bar and broke it. Inside were shiny crystals of sugar with gas bubbles in between (Fig a). Liz said, 'This is how rocks are made.' She took a piece of rock out of her pocket and held it up. 'Look! You can see the crystals and the bubbles,' she said.

Tom said, 'Don't be silly! Rocks aren't made in factories — they come out of the Earth!'

Lotti had a pocket book on 'Rocks' with her. 'Look at this picture of a volcano,' she said. 'Don't you think it's rather like the sweet bar factory?'

'What do you mean?' said Tom.

'Well, red hot lava pours out of the volcano with gases under a lot of pressure. Then when the lava cools down to make a rock, the gas bubbles are trapped.'

'Just like the sweet bar,' said Liz. 'Ugh! But it doesn't taste as good!'

A

B Liz's rock — a basalt with gas bubbles.

C A hardened lava flow.

This is what Lotti's book said:

> **Igneous** rocks are made from molten **magma**. This may cool slowly below ground to form a rock with large crystals. If the magma reaches the surface in a lava flow, it will cool much more quickly to form smaller crystals.

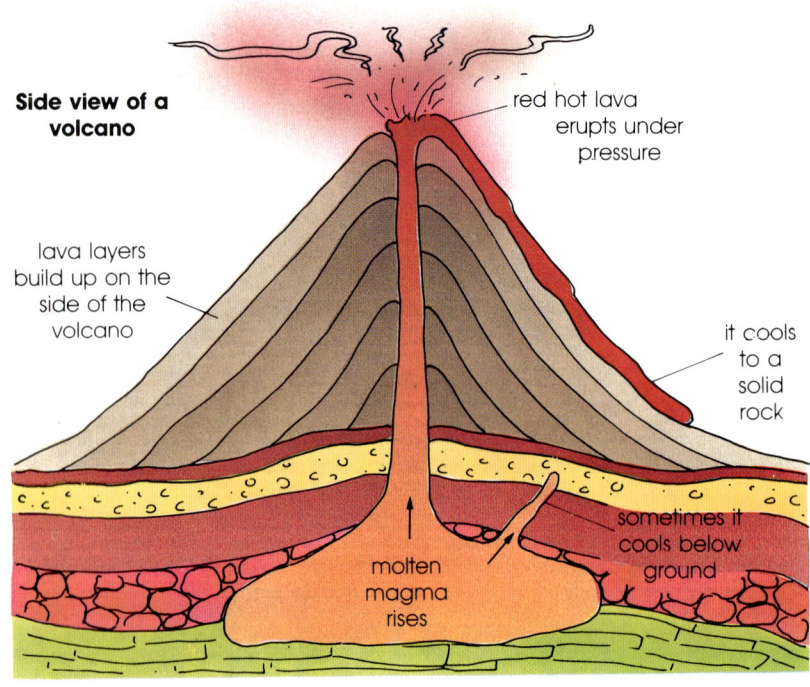

Side view of a volcano

red hot lava erupts under pressure

lava layers build up on the side of the volcano

it cools to a solid rock

molten magma rises

sometimes it cools below ground

D Page from Lotti's book.

Activity 2.1

When Tom got home he decided to make some crystals of his own. He found these instructions in a science book but he had some trouble following them. Can you help him?

Crystals

50 ml water (3 tablespoons)
about 25 ml salt
Warm water in a pan. Stir in table salt until no more will dissolve. Bring to the boil. Then pour the liquid into a dish and allow to cool.

MAKING BIGGER CRYSTALS

Choose a well-shaped crystal and suspend it in a jar of salt solution. Leave the crystal to 'grow' for several days.

1 What equipment would Tom need to measure out the water and salt?
2 What will happen to the salt as it is heated and stirred?
3 How will Tom know when the water has come to the boil?
4 Tom poured some of the water into a saucer, the rest he left in a pan. Where do you think the first crystals would form — in the saucer or the pan?
5 What shape would the crystals be?
6 If more time is allowed for the crystals to form, do you get bigger or smaller crystals?
7 When Tom got back to school his teacher showed **(WP)** him two pieces of igneous rock, like the ones in Figs e and f. The teacher said, 'Both of these rocks were once a red hot liquid — do you know which rock cooled slowly and which cooled fast?' Because of Tom's work on crystals, he was able to answer the question correctly. What do you think his answer was? Can you explain his answer?

Now try these

1 Make a copy of Fig d. On your copy label where you think granite and basalt would have formed.
2 Fig g is a photograph of a rock called obsidian. This rock is a natural glass. It cooled so quickly that crystals did not have time to form. Label on your diagram where you think this rock would have formed.
3 Examine other samples of igneous rock and make sketches of them.

E Granite

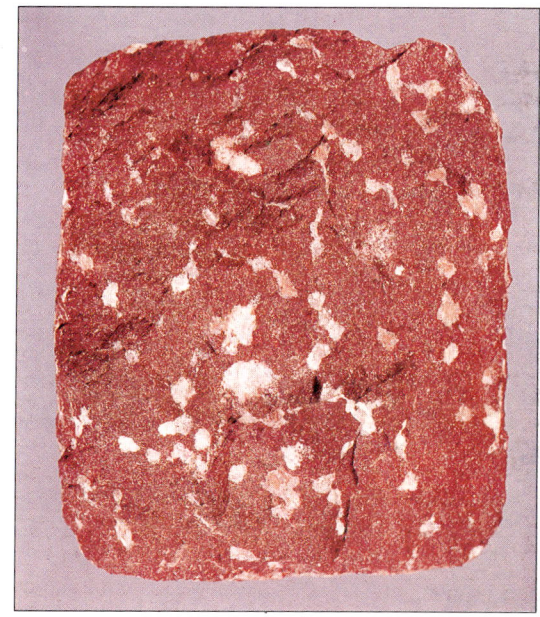

F Basalt lava

G Obsidian

ROCKS AND WEATHERING

2.2 Finding out more about rocks

Have you ever noticed the variety of pebbles on a beach (Fig a)? Not only are the pebbles different shapes and sizes, but they have different colours. Some are harder or smoother than others. Beach pebbles are loose fragments of rock. They have not always been lying on a beach. Where did they come from?

A

Try this

Answer these questions about beach pebbles. If possible look at samples of pebbles collected from a beach. For each question, choose the most likely answer in the brackets.

1 What shape are most pebbles? (rectangular/rounded)
2 What could have happened to change their shape over many years? (wave action/bad weather)
3 How did beach pebbles get onto a beach in the first place? (broken off cliffs/washed down by rivers/thrown there by people/carried there by big storm waves)

Lotti, Liz and Tom decided to go and collect some rocks. 'Where should we look?' asked Liz.

'I'm going to begin in that road cutting,' said Tom.

'And there's that dried out river bed,' said Lotti.

'Listen to what it says here,' said Liz, reading out of her book.

The best places to look for rocks are areas where the earth has been disturbed or worn away by water or wind. Sea cliffs, fields, wasteground and even gardens are all good places to search. Be very careful when collecting rocks. Don't go near overhanging cliffs or climb rock faces. Avoid quarries which may be dangerous.

How to work

Before you collect rock samples record what you see. If you have a camera take photographs. Note down the exact details of the place you are visiting. Also make notes and sketches about where you found the rock. Take labelled plastic bags with you. Put one rock sample into each bag. Write on the label where the rock came from and what you think it is.

Activity 2.2

Looking at a pebble rock
A rock made of pebbles is called a **conglomerate** (Fig b). Look at a sample of conglomerate and compare it with a loose collection of pebbles.

1 Does the rock look the same as the pebbles?
2 How is the rock different from the pebbles?
3 What can you see in between the pebbles in the rock holding the pebbles together?
4 Make a sketch of the loose pebbles and the conglomerate.

B Conglomerate: what holds the pebbles together?

notebook

a geological hammer

safety goggles to avoid rock splinters

labelled plastic bags

C Equipment for collecting rock samples.

Activity 2.3

Looking at other rocks

Bring a rock sample into school. Look in places suggested by Liz's book.

1 The rock you choose may have a surface that is dirty, pitted or altered by the weather. If so, then wrap your sample in a cloth and strike it with a hammer. You will be able to see freshly broken surfaces. Compare these with the weather-worn outside of the rock.

2 Look at your sample rock and compare it with at least five other samples brought in by your friends (see Fig d). Use a hand lens for magnifying any tiny features you can see. To find out how hard the rocks are you could use a bronze coin and a large pin for scratching (always scratch away from you).

3 Write down the results of your tests on a chart like **(SS)** the one shown in Fig e, using these questions:
   - What colour is it?
   - Is it shiny?
   - Does it break easily?
   - Does it scratch easily? (Write down 'hard' or 'soft'.)
   - What does it smell like?
   - What does it feel like?
   - Does it soak up water?
   - Does it fizz with dilute hydrochloric acid?
   - What does it look like? (sketch)

D Look at the samples carefully. Use a hand lens to examine tiny features.

Activity 2.4

Comparing rocks

Sort out all the rocks brought in by you and your friends into groups according to their colour, hardness or other differences. How many groups have you divided them into? Sketch one interesting rock from each group.

ROCK CHART

ROCK TYPE? igneous   NAME? granite

WHAT COLOUR? — The rock is a speckled grey colour.

IS IT SHINY? — No, it is dull looking.

DOES IT BREAK EASILY? — No.

Sketch of rock sample

E

The three main rock types

Rocks are divided into three groups according to how they were formed. There are many varieties of each type.

- **Igneous** From volcanoes and underground, molten magma. These rocks are usually quite hard and made of crystals.
- **Sedimentary** Rock fragments laid down in layers, sometimes containing fossil evidence of early life. They have formed from the wearing away of previous rocks.
- **Metamorphic** Rocks altered by heat and pressure deep inside the Earth. They may later come to the surface because of Earth movements.

Now try this

Re-sort your samples into igneous, sedimentary and metamorphic groups. Then find out the *names* of your samples and list them under each heading.

ROCKS AND WEATHERING

2.3 How rocks change through weathering

Lotti was helping her dad replace some crumbling bricks on their house. She said, 'You wouldn't think something as hard as a brick would start to crumble. . . I wonder why it's happened?' Can you answer Lotti's question?

Later that day, Lotti, Liz and Tom were playing in the old churchyard. 'Look at that old stone carving,' said Liz. 'It's all crumbling away.'

'And these gravestones,' said Tom. 'This one says 185. . . something. I can't read it.'

'You can read this one,' said Lotti. 'This person died in 1950.'

'I wonder how long it takes for stones to crumble away?' said Tom.

'There's something in my book on that,' said Lotti . . .

Weathering

All rocks slowly crumble away when they are exposed to the air (Fig a). Changes in wind, rain and temperature can attack the rocks. The crumbling process is called **weathering**. For most rocks, this is a very slow process taking thousands of years, but some rocks can weather much more quickly. It all depends on the kind of rock and where it is.

Frost damage

If water gets into cracks and then freezes, it will turn to ice inside the crack. Ice takes up more space than water. Ice pressure will make the crack bigger and wider. On a mountain side, a rock face will start to crumble. The loosened rocks will fall down and pile up as **scree** at the foot of the slope (Fig b).

Water damage

Rain can soak into a rock and find its way between the rock grains. It will dissolve the cement holding the grains together. Then the rock will start to crumble.

When raindrops fall through the air, they pick up carbon dioxide. This turns rainwater into a weak acid. If the rainwater then soaks through the soil, more acids will dissolve and be picked up.

A Old bricks.   New bricks.

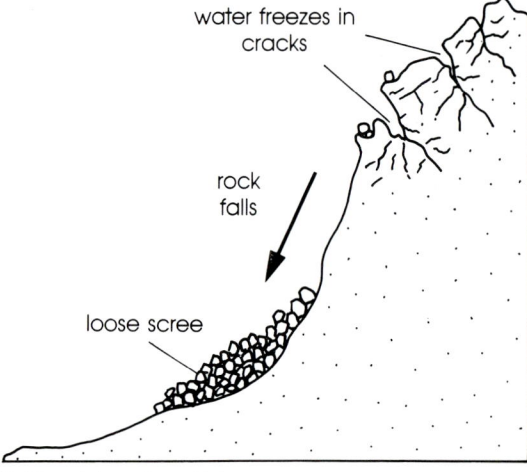

water freezes in cracks

rock falls

loose scree

B 'Crumble and tumble'.

C How Ghyll, North Yorks: a dry valley in limestone. Where has the water gone?

The weathering of limestone

Limestone is a sedimentary rock which is dissolved easily by rainwater (Fig c). Rainwater widens surface cracks in limestone. It is easy for water to soak into the rock along these cracks. Therefore underground streams are very common. In limestone areas there is very little surface water. Underground caverns are sometimes hollowed out as rainwater passes through the limestone (Fig d). These caverns can be huge. The Carlsbad Cavern in New Mexico, USA is 1200 metres long and 90 metres high.

D A cave hollowed out of limestone. The icicle-like stalactites form as water drips from the roof.

Activity 2.6

Is limestone dissolved by a weak acid?

Add a small piece of limestone to each test tube (see Fig e). Watch for a few minutes to see what happens. Then write down what you have found out to answer this question.

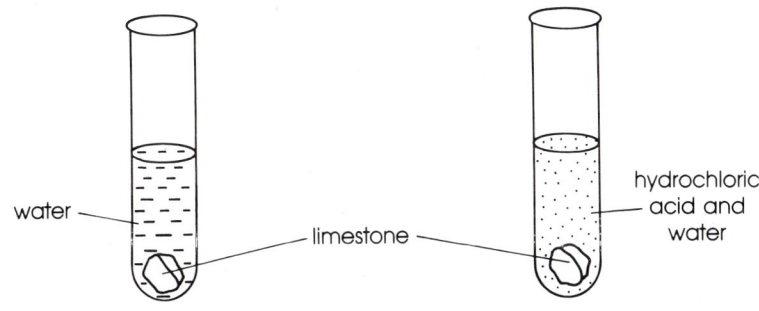

water — limestone — hydrochloric acid and water

E Is limestone dissolved?

Activity 2.5

How does ice pressure crumble rocks?

Fill a glass bottle with water, cork and seal it carefully inside a plastic bag in the freezer. When it is frozen re-examine it. What has happened to the bottle?

Now try these

1 Why did Tom have so much trouble reading the date in the graveyard?
2 What is the name for the crumbling process that affects rocks?
3 What might have caused the bricks on Lotti's house to crumble?
4 How does frost damage affect **a** buildings made of stone and brick, **b** rocks in the landscape?
5 From the activities you have done, explain how water can make rocks crumble and dissolve away.
6 This is what a pupil wrote **(WP)** about an area of limestone scenery. Rewrite the report, choosing the correct words from the brackets:

   The hills and valleys all look very (dry/wet). The valleys (have/haven't) streams at the bottom. Rivers run (underground/above ground). The soil is very (thick/thin). The surface rocks have (narrow/wide) cracks, and there are (caves/no caves).

7 Do your own detective work like Tom and his friends in your nearest churchyard or cemetery. Note down the oldest dates you can read. Is there any pattern to these dates? For example, are the older gravestones made of particular rock types like granite? Are the stones less weathered in sheltered places?

ROCKS AND WEATHERING

2.4 Erosion

Did you know that the rocks of the Earth are under continuous attack? Weathering makes the rocks soften and crumble away. At the same time, wind, rivers, ice and sea waves can wear away huge amounts of surface rock — a process called **erosion**.

It was the holidays and Tom's dad had taken the children to Edinburgh Castle in Scotland. 'What a great place to build a castle,' said Tom.

'Right on top of a huge rock,' said Liz.

'Did you know that it was once a volcano?' said Lotti, opening her book on 'Rocks'. 'It says that all the softer ash and lava on the sides of the cone have gone. Only the hard rock that was once the volcano's central pipe is still here.' (See Fig a.)

'I wonder what happened to the sides of the volcano?' said Tom, looking puzzled.

Try this

What is the answer to Tom's question? See what it says in Lotti's book below. It may help you.

At the same time as rocks are being softened by weathering, the rocks are being worn away by erosion. Erosion can involve the movement of rock fragments in a number of different ways:

- by gravity down a slope
- by streams and rivers
- by ice
- by wind
- by sea waves and tidal movements.

Movement of loose sand and pebbles can itself cause more erosion. For example, a river uses the pebbles it carries to cut a deeper and wider river bed. Eventually a V-shaped valley is formed (Fig b).

In cold climates, ice sheets and glaciers have rocks embedded on their undersides. As they move, they scrape over the land like huge sheets of sandpaper and remove vast amounts of rock fragments (Fig c).

In dry climates, wind will pick up dust and sand. When the sand is blown against bare rocks it can wear away the softer layers, especially near to the ground (see Fig d).

Waves will pick up pebbles and hurl them against the foot of a cliff, breaking off more rock fragments (see Fig e).

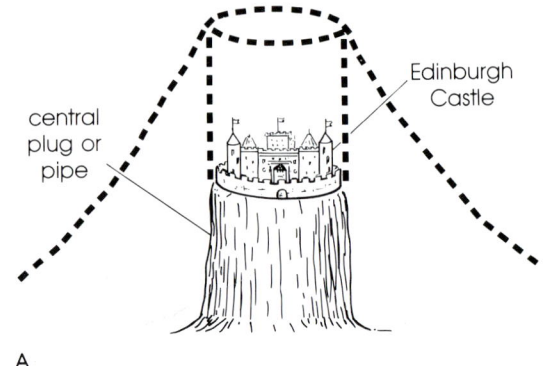

A

B The Colorado River has cut through 3000 metres of rock in 21 million years to make the Grand Canyon.

C Huge, moving lumps of ice called glaciers carve out deep valleys as they move slowly downhill.

What happens to all this loose rock material? Most erosion takes place where rocks are most exposed, in high mountains. Because of gravity, most of the eroded material comes to rest either on lowland or on the sea floor. Ice sheets and rivers flow downhill to the sea, carrying pebbles, sand and mud – all of which have come from the erosion of rocks.

E Sliddey Cove, Co. Antrim. What part of the cliff is hit most by waves? Why has the arch formed?

Deposition

When all the rock fragments come to rest they form layers of **sediment**. Rivers carry so much material from the land towards the sea that the sea floor is where most of the new rock layers form. These layers form the sedimentary rocks. In time, the layers harden as they are buried beneath newer layers.

Now try these

1 Write out the following statements and say next to each one whether they are *true* or *false*.
   a Erosion is the process that wears away rocks.
   b Only soft rocks are worn away.
   c All erosion involves the movement of rock material.
   d New sediments only form on the sea bed.
   e Volcanoes are made of such hard rock that they never erode away.
   f Rivers erode their banks most at bends.
2 What about Tom's problem with the Edinburgh **WP** volcano? Even though the volcano is over 300 million years old, some of it still remains. It takes millions of years for the fragments from a volcano to settle on the sea floor and become sedimentary rock. Write a report to Tom explaining what might have happened to the Edinburgh volcano.

D A rock pedestal: often seen in hot deserts.

Activity 2.7

Rivers at work

For this activity you need a stream tray, at least 20 cm by 30 cm and about 8 cm deep. This could be made of wood or plastic.

Set up the sloping tray so that the outlet hole is over a sink (Fig f). Fill the top end of the tray with damp sand. Trickle water from a length of tubing onto a bottle top.

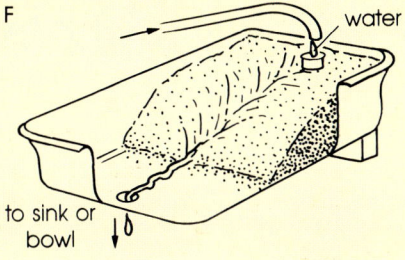

F

Try to answer these questions:
1 How does the 'river' erode the sand?
2 What happens at bends in the 'river'?
3 Does a 'valley' form and what is the shape of the valley that the 'river' erodes?
4 Did any of the sand move? If so, where?
5 What happens at the mouth of the 'river'?

There are many variations to this activity that you could try. For example, what happens if you heighten or lower the slope? What happens if you add gravel to the sand?

ROCKS AND WEATHERING

2.5 Down a mine

Lotti, Liz and Tom were very excited. They were going on a school visit to a coal mine. To get down to where the coal was being mined they had to be lowered 100 metres down a shaft in a cage (Fig a). Tom slipped and dirtied his clothes on the black coal dust. 'Anyway, why do we need coal?' he said, sounding annoyed. 'It's of no use to me!'

Lotti was reading a leaflet about the mine. 'You couldn't be more wrong,' she said. 'Look at what it says here in my leaflet.'

'I didn't realise we all use coal every day of our lives!' said Tom. 'Come on,' he said, 'the others will be ages. Let's get in.' He pulled a lever and the cage suddenly speeded up and dropped down the shaft. They all began to scream. Eventually, the cage slowed down and finally stopped. To their surprise, they stepped out into a tropical rainforest. It was so hot, smelly and swampy that it was difficult to walk. They were clambering over slippery, fallen logs that were sinking into the swamp. 'Look,' said Lotti, 'What is that?'

It's a huge dragonfly,' said Liz. 'You know, I think we've gone back in time!'

'Yes,' said Tom. 'These trees are sinking into this black, peaty swamp and it will all turn into coal one day!'

'I can't see how that could happen,' said Lotti. 'It's all too wet and sludgy and it doesn't look at all like coal.'

Liz said, 'You haven't read the second page of your leaflet, Lotti. That tells you how it happens. . .'

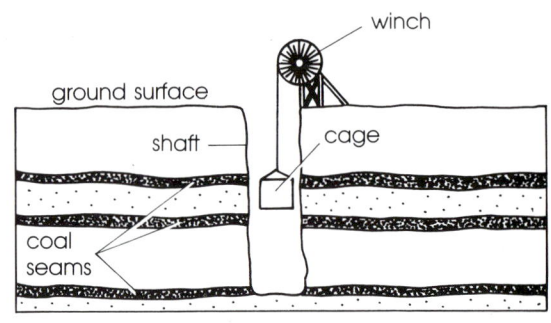

A

THE USES OF COAL

Coal contains hydrocarbons. These can be used to make plastics, fertilisers and even perfumes (see Fig b). The main use for coal is as a fuel. Burning coal provides energy for industry. Power stations use coal – burning coal heats steam which drives the fan blades of turbines to make electricity.

B

C Life in the Carboniferous period about 300 million years ago.

THE HISTORY OF COAL

Dead, decaying plant matter collected as layers of peat in swamps. In Britain this happened in the Carboniferous period – 300 million years ago. As time passed, the peat layers became buried by layers of sand and mud brought down by rivers. Sometimes the sea flooded the area. Then a new swamp formed, only to be buried again. This happened several times. Then the water was squeezed out by pressure, and the peat slowly turned into coal. It took about 100 million years for a thick layer of peat to become a coal seam. (See Fig e.)

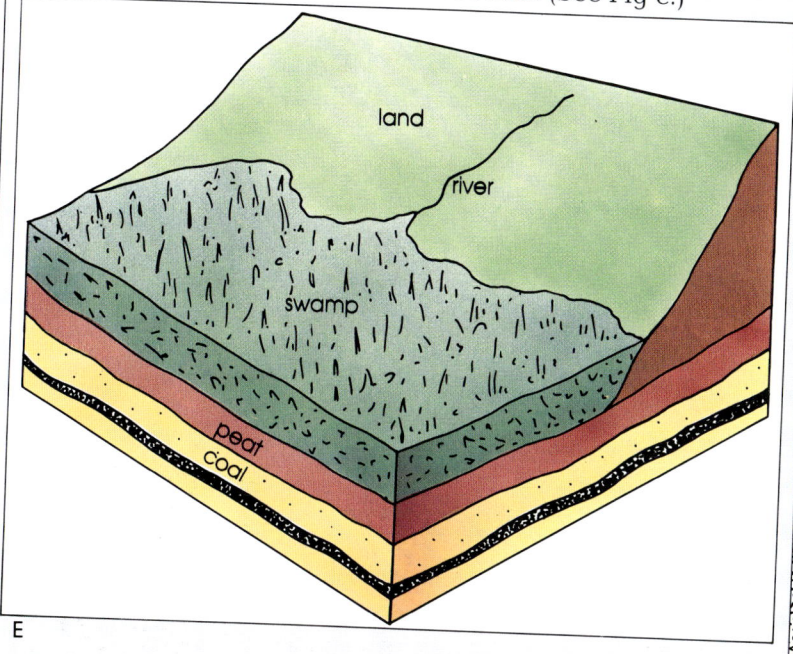

E

D A fossil leaf.

'This place gives me the creeps,' said Lotti. 'Let's go back.' The cage rose up the shaft to the surface. They could hear their teacher and the other children coming towards them. Strangely, their adventure didn't seem to have taken more than a second or two of real time!

Activity 2.8

Is coal a different rock?

1 Work in pairs to examine a piece of coal and compare it with other rocks, eg shale or limestone. Write down some notes about what it is like:
   - Is it hard or soft?
   - What colour is it?
   - Is it dusty or clean?
2 Compare what you have written with another pair. Have you thought of the same things?
3 Using tongs, hold a piece of coal in the flame of a **(G)** Bunsen burner. What happens? Try this with other rocks.

Now try these

1 What is another name for layers of coal?
2 What is the first stage in the formation of coal? (Read about the children's adventure, and the second page of Lotti's leaflet to find this out.)
3 Liz said that they 'had gone back in time'. Why did she think this?
4 What was it that Lotti didn't understand about coal?
5 Write a note to Lotti explaining how peat turns into coal. (Use the second page of the leaflet to help you.)
6 Write a report with this **(WP)** heading: 'How coal is different from other rocks'. Write down your main findings.
7 How did the rock layers form that are sandwiched between each coal layer?
8 Make a poster to show the **(DTP)** uses of coal.
9 Examine a block of peat and compare it with the coal sample you have seen.

ROCKS AND WEATHERING

2.6 Changes in rock layers 1

'I can see how sloppy sediment can collect in layers,' said Liz, 'but how does it turn to solid rock?'

'Well, just think of those coal seams,' said Tom, 'and the weight of all those rocks on top pushing down on them.'

'Does it say anything in your book, Lotti?' asked Liz.

'Yes,' said Lotti, 'but I'm not sure what it means. . .' This is what Lotti's book said:

Try this

Explain to Lotti what happens. What else, apart from pressure, is helping to make the rocks go hard?

How sediment becomes solid rock

Layers of loose sediment become buried by new layers. The weight helps to squeeze the rock grains closer together — a process called **compaction** (Fig a). Minerals are left as a coating around the rock grains and they act as a cement, holding the grains together — a process called **cementation** (Fig b).

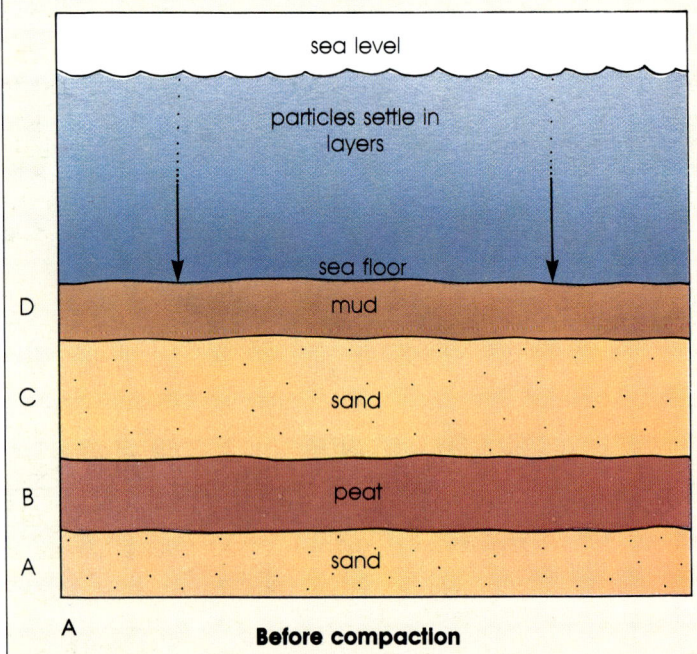

Before compaction

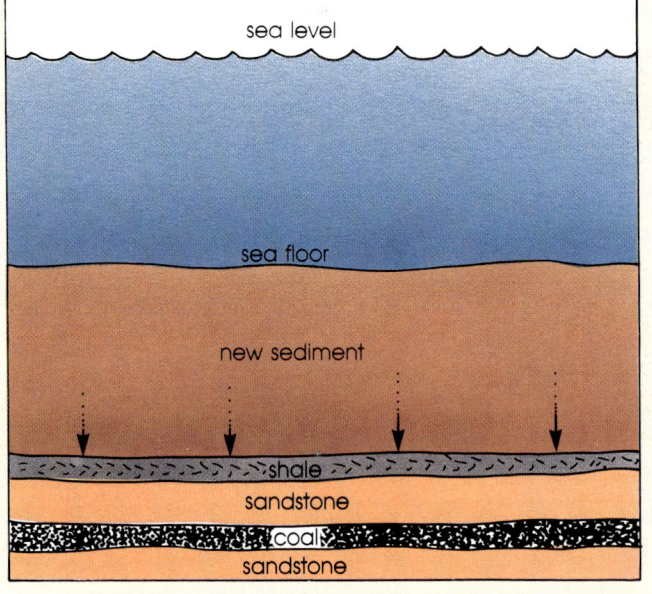

After compaction

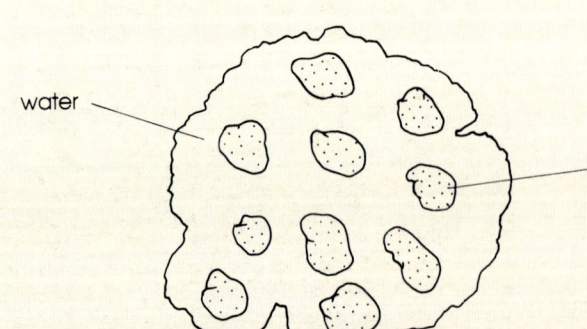

Before

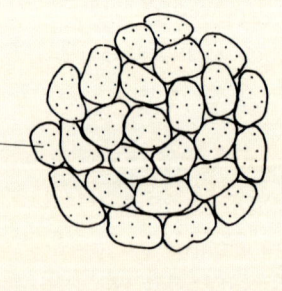

After

Activity 2.9

Making compacted rocks

For this activity you need a 5 ml disposable syringe with the end cut off using a hacksaw (Fig c). Spread a little petroleum jelly inside the syringe. Pull the plunger to the top of the syringe and fill the syringe with damp sand. Seal the open end of the syringe with your finger and press down the plunger to squeeze the sand (Fig d). Then push out the sand 'rock' onto a piece of paper (Fig e).

1 What does your 'rock' look like under the microscope?
2 How do the sand grains pack together?
3 Gently nip the 'rock' between your finger and thumb. Is it hard or soft?

You made this 'rock' by pressing the sand grains together. In a natural rock the grains are usually cemented together by various materials.

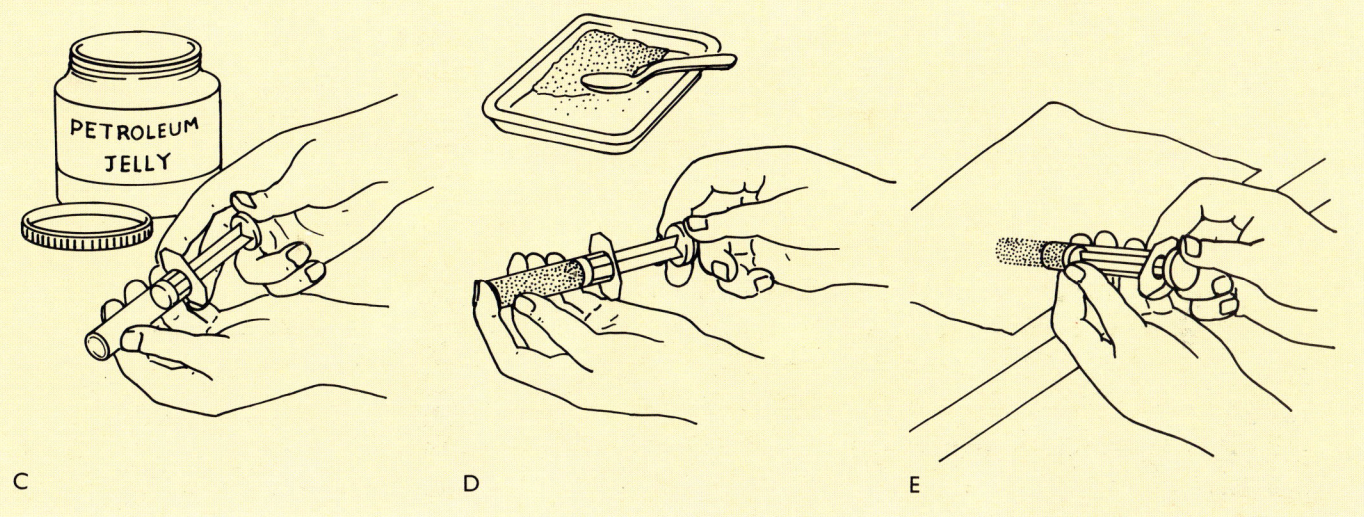

C   D   E

Activity 2.10

Making cemented rocks

1 Repeat Activity 2.9 but each time try mixing sand with different solutions and powders. If you are working with a group of friends you could each try a different cement and compare your results. You could use:
   - salt solution
   - sugar solution
   - iron sulphate solution
   - Polyfilla powder
   - clay.
2 Label each rock sample and note down the cement you used.
3 Allow the squeezed out 'rocks' to set and dry over several hours. Compare the 'rocks' you have made with the compacted 'rocks' you made in Activity 2.9. Are they harder or softer?
4 Which of the 'rocks' makes the hardest sandstone?
5 Compare your artificial 'rocks' with real sandstones. In what ways are they the same or different?

Now try these

1 Write a letter to Lotti **WP** explaining what happens when sloppy mud and sand is turned to solid rock.
2 What substance is lost as the rock grains are squeezed closer together?
3 Copy this passage and fill in **WP** the gaps using the words below.

each; loose; called; layers; grains; rock; compaction.

Layers of _____ sediment are buried by newer _____. The weight presses the _____ grains closer together. This process is called _____. Minerals are left coating the _____. This makes them stick to _____ other. This process is _____ **cementation**.

ROCKS AND WEATHERING

2.7 Layered rocks

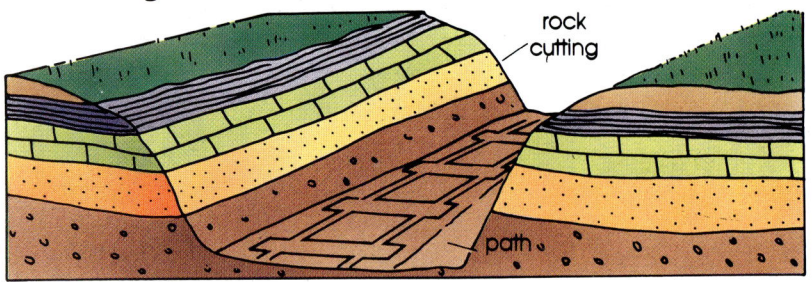

A

After school, Lotti, Tom and Liz decided to walk along the path next to the disused railway line (Fig a). The path took them through a cutting and they could see layers of rock on either side. 'Look!' said Liz. 'It's just like the layers we saw in the coal mine,' and she stopped to take photographs of them.

Tom bent down to have a closer look at the bottom layer. 'This one looks like a layer of concrete,' he said. 'It's made of lots of pebbles cemented together.' (You can see a picture of the rock Tom found in Fig b on page 24.)

'This one over here is strange,' said Lotti. 'You can see sand grains in it and they are all stuck together.'

'The rock I've picked up has got seashells in it and it's a creamy colour,' said Liz.

As they walked further on, Tom found another rock. 'This is a different one,' he said. 'You can see flaky layers in it and it looks like black mud that has been pressed together and hardened.'

'Let's find out more about them,' said Lotti, and she got out her pocket book on 'Rocks'. Look at the opposite page to find out what Lotti's book said, and to see the three photographs which Liz took.

Activity 2.11

Making layered rocks

Try to think of a way of testing how the sediments settle in layers. You can use gravel, sand, clay, water and a watertight bottle.

In pairs, first work out a method of doing the experiment. You will need to decide how much sand, gravel and clay to use. Compare your method with other pairs. Write down and sketch what happens as the sediment settles.

1 Does the sediment form clear layers? Make a labelled sketch of what you see.
2 How long does it take for the heavier material to settle?
3 How long does it take for the fine mud to settle?

Now try these

1 Which is the oldest layer of rock that the children found?
2 Why do pebbles settle near to the shore?
3 In Activity 2.11, which sediment settles out first?
4 In Activity 2.11, how much time does it take for each layer to settle?
5 When the rock layers in the railway cutting were deposited, was the sea getting shallower, deeper or staying about the same?

Puzzle

When the children got home they tried to match up Liz's photographs of the rocks with the rock samples they had picked up, and with the notes in Lotti's book. 'I can't work this out,' said Tom. 'I think we need some help.' Can you help them sort out their rocks?

1 Work in pairs and look carefully at:
  • the four samples: limestone, shale, sandstone and conglomerate
  • the three photographs that Liz took and Fig b on page 24
  • what the children said about the four rocks
  • the page from Lotti's book on 'Rocks'.
2 Try to match up the rock samples and photographs with what the children said about them and the descriptions from the book.
3 Set out a report on your rocks (SS) like this:

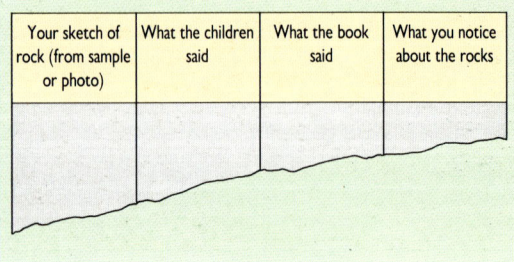

Your sketch of rock (from sample or photo)	What the children said	What the book said	What you notice about the rocks

Layered rocks

Rocks found in layers are called **sedimentary rocks**. They form from sediments like sand, mud and silt. This material is carried by wind and water currents, until it finally settles in layers (Fig e). Most sediments start as sloppy mud or loose sand, collecting on the sea bed or at the bottom of lakes and rivers. Pebbles and gravel carried by rivers or by shoreline waves settle out quickly because they are heavy. They eventually form a rock called a **conglomerate**. Sand will settle further out from the shore to form **sandstone** (Fig b). Mud and silt particles may be carried some distance from the land and then settle to form mudstone or **shale** (Fig c). The fragments of shells, corals and other sea creatures collect as a limey mud on the sea bed to form a rock called **limestone** (Fig d).

B Sandstone.

C Shale.

D Limestone.

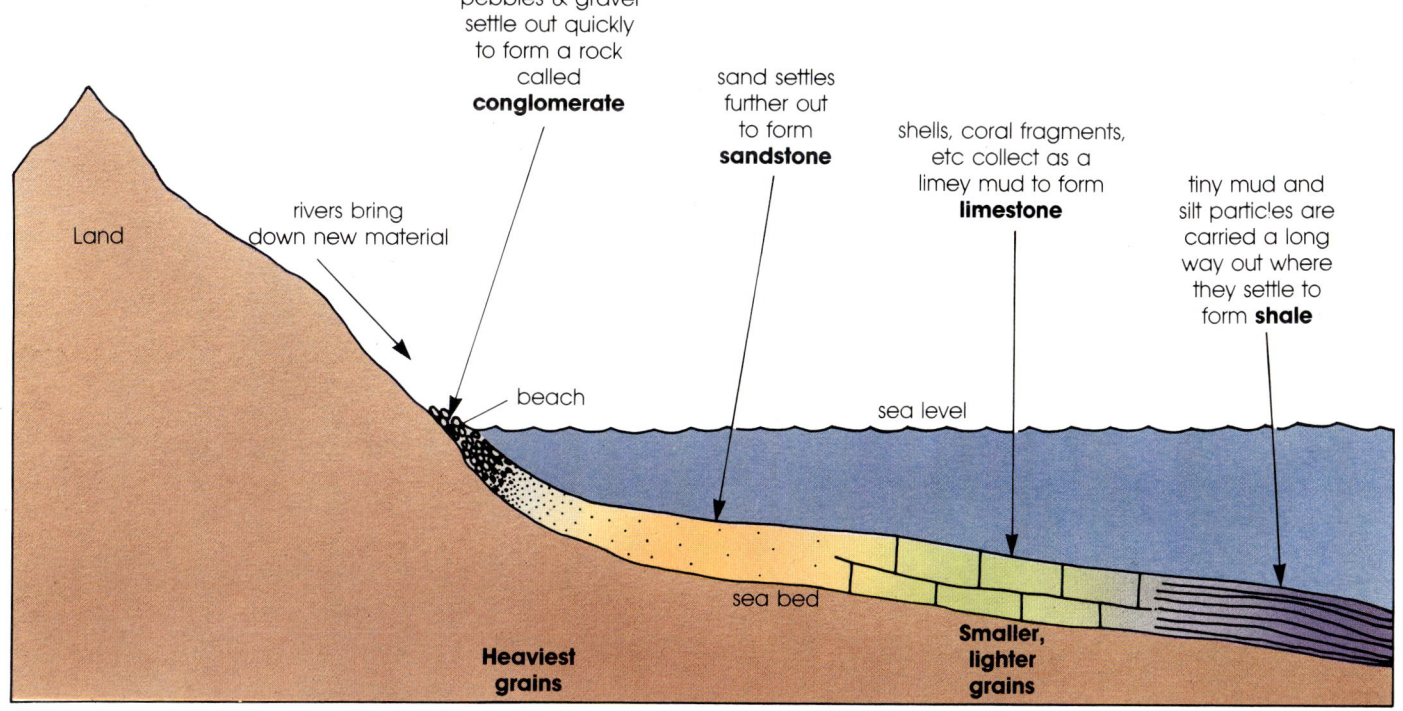

pebbles & gravel settle out quickly to form a rock called **conglomerate**

sand settles further out to form **sandstone**

shells, coral fragments, etc collect as a limey mud to form **limestone**

tiny mud and silt particles are carried a long way out where they settle to form **shale**

rivers bring down new material

Land

beach

sea level

sea bed

Heaviest grains

Smaller, lighter grains

E

ROCKS AND WEATHERING

2.8 Sediments and fossils

Do you know what fossils are and how fossils are made? Do you want to try making some yourself?

First read about how fossils are found. . .
Lotti, Liz and Tom were fed up. There was nothing on TV and it was raining again. Tom was reading the newspaper. 'Just listen to this,' said Tom.

'Oh no!' said Liz. 'Newspapers are so boring.'

'This isn't,' said Tom. 'There's been a new dinosaur find.'

Lotti grabbed the newspaper from him. 'It's near here,' she said. 'In the quarry on Fossil Knoll Hill.'

This is what she read out. . .

New dinosaur 'rocks' the experts

A TEENAGE fossil hunter has shaken the world's dinosaur experts. Gavin came across the hind leg of a dinosaur in a cliff face. Experts think that the bones belong to hypsilophodon, a 2-legged creature, 17 feet long which lived 120 million years ago. Until Gavin found his fossil bones these dinosaurs were thought to grow only seven feet long.

'It's stopped raining,' Lotti said. 'Let's go and have a look.' When they got to the quarry there were bones lying everywhere.

'I don't understand why these bones are still here,' said Tom. 'Why haven't they rotted away?'

'I can answer that,' said Lotti. 'Listen to what it says in my fossil book. . .

How fossils were made

When plants and animals die they usually get eaten or they rot away. Sometimes they can be quickly buried by layers of sand and mud (Fig c, stage 1). Then the plant or animal has a chance of being preserved. Even after burial the softer parts will rot, but sometimes the hard parts, such as shell, bone and wood in plants, become replaced. Chemicals carried by water seep into the fossil and slowly turn it to stone (Fig c, stage 2). After a very long time, movements in the Earth tilt and fold the rock layers. The rocks are lifted to the surface. Wind and rain wear the rocks away and uncover the fossil (stage 3).

Try this

Fossils give us clues to what animals and plants were like. Fig a shows a dinosaur skeleton. Can you make a sketch of the animal with flesh on its bones? If you can, you have used the fossil clues correctly.

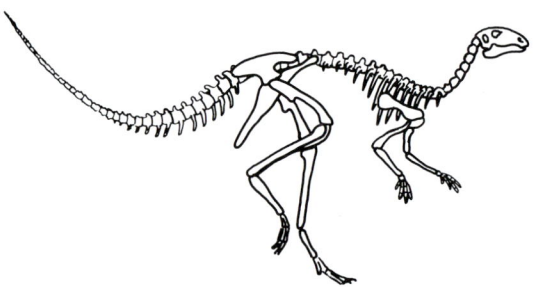

A

B Gavin with the reconstructed leg of the giant dinosaur.

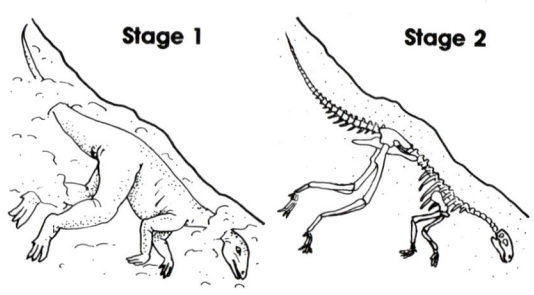

Stage 1   Stage 2

C

Activity 2.12

1 Tom did not understand why the fossil bones were **WP** still there after so long. Write a note to Tom explaining why.

2 What clues tell the experts that the dinosaur was 2-legged and 17 feet long?

3 The fossils were found lying at the surface. What had happened to uncover the fossils? Draw a sketch to show this third stage.

Activity 2.13

Making fossil teeth and nails

Fossils of dinosaur footprints are often found. The print shows the shape of the foot. You can make fossils like this using modelling clay and plaster (Fig e).

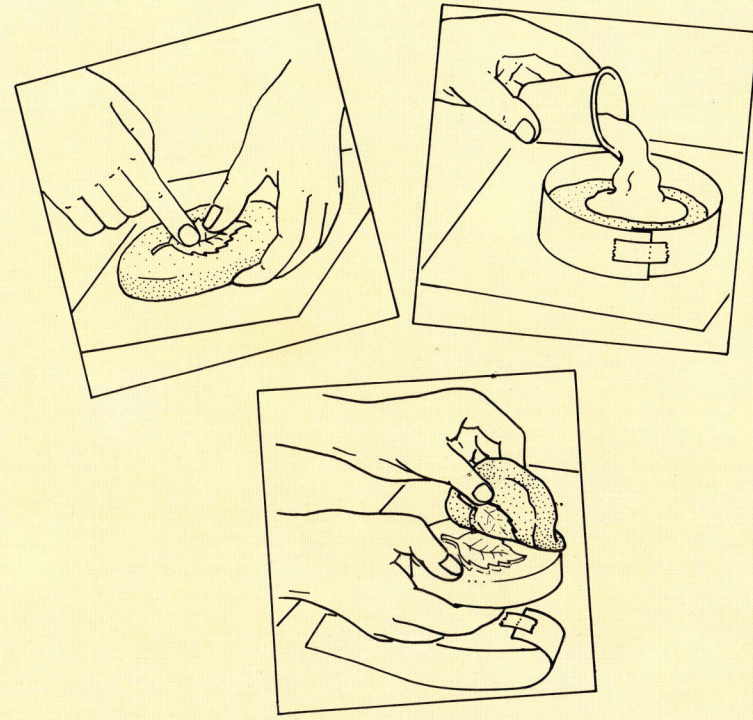

E

First flatten the modelling clay and press a 'fossil' into the clay. You could use leaves, tree bark, shells — even your own teeth or fingernails. When you have removed the fossil place a card cylinder round the modelling clay. Mix some dental plaster, slowly adding water until it is a creamy mixture. Pour the mixture onto the print of the fossil. Leave it to set. Then peel off the modelling clay. Look at the fossil you have made.

How many different fossils did the group make? Make a list of the animals and plants everyone used.

What did dinosaurs eat?

Dinosaur skulls are important clues to what the animals ate. Look at Fig d. From what you know of animals today, which one was a meat-eater and which was a plant-eater?

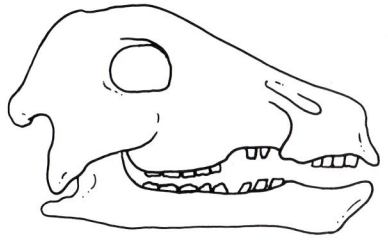

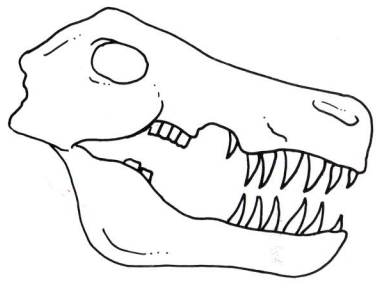

D

Now try these

1 Write out the following **WP** sentences choosing the correct word or phrase from the brackets.

a The soft parts of a dinosaur are (more/less) likely to become a fossil.

b Fossils are more likely to form from animals that (lived on land/lived on the sea floor).

c Animals *with* bones are (more/less) likely to turn into fossils.

d Because the dead animal or plant is replaced by chemicals, the original colour of the animal or plant is (lost/preserved).

2 What are the chances of **WP** material becoming a fossil? Put this list into order, starting with the item most likely to become a fossil: egg shell; thigh bone; slug; snail; leaf; earthworm; mussel shell; sea anenome; tree trunk.

ROCKS AND WEATHERING

2.9 Metamorphic rocks

Would you like to be harder, stronger and more powerful? Wonderwoman and Superman can do it! So can caterpillars when they want to be butterflies. All you need to do is to 'change your form'. In rocks, this process is called **metamorphism** (change form). 'Meta' is a Greek word meaning 'change'. 'Morphe' means 'form'.

Rocks have been doing this for millions of years. Did you know that if a chocolate biscuit is put under enough pressure it will change into a diamond? Both are made of a material called carbon — the difference is that the carbon atoms in a diamond are much closer together than in a chocolate biscuit.

Tom and Liz were watching Lotti in the kitchen. She was busy mixing the ingredients for a cake. 'Isn't it strange. . .!' said Liz.

'Isn't what strange?' asked Tom impatiently.

'Well, how that white mixture comes out of the oven looking and tasting completely different.'

'So what,' said Tom, 'it's called baking, isn't it?'

'But don't you see?' said Liz. 'It's a kind of metamorphism. The cake mix is changed by heat into something else.'

'Here is one I made earlier,' said Lotti. 'But it's not a rock cake! Liz, see what it says in my book on 'Rocks'.

This is what Liz read. . .

A Why is it unusual to find fossils in metamorphic rocks like this one?

B Metamorphic rock often has a banded appearance.

A metamorphic rock is formed when heat and/or pressure causes rocks to change. The chemicals inside a rock react and re-form into new minerals. The heat changes are not caused by the rock melting. If this happened, then new magma and igneous rocks would form instead.

Where does the pressure and heat come from?
Underground rocks come under intense pressure when fold mountains are made. Underground rocks that are near to molten magma beneath volcanoes can be baked by the heat from the magma as it cools.

Metamorphic rocks rarely contain fossils because these are destroyed as the rock re-forms. Metamorphic rocks often have a banded or striped appearance (Fig b). They often have a crystal structure which makes them generally hard and strong. Some examples of metamorphic changes are shown in the table opposite.

Main cause	Original rock	Metamorphic rock
heat	limestone	marble
heat	sandstone	meta-quartzite
heat and pressure	mudstone and shale	schist or gneiss
pressure	mudstone and shale	slate

Activity 2.14

Looking at changes in rocks

Study samples of the nine different rocks mentioned in the table. Use a 2p coin and your fingernail to test for hardness. Compare the rock samples in each pair as shown below. Write down your findings in a table like this one:

	Sedimentary	Metamorphic
Can you scratch the rock with your fingernail or the coin?		
Write down the colour of the rock.		
What does the rock feel like? (Is it rough, smooth, gritty, etc?)		
Does it break easily into layers?		

Uses of metamorphic rocks and minerals

There are many uses for metamorphic materials (see Fig c).

Slate is often used, especially in older buildings. Marble is sometimes used as an ornamental facing stone on city buildings like banks and offices. Asbestos is still used to insulate some buildings. It is a mineral made of fibres which can be woven into cloth or pressed into sheets. Powdered asbestos can be very dangerous, causing lung damage if breathed in, so it has to be handled very carefully. Talc is another metamorphic mineral. It is easily powdered and scented to make talcum powder. It is also used to make the moving parts of machines more slippery in cases where oil or grease cannot be used.

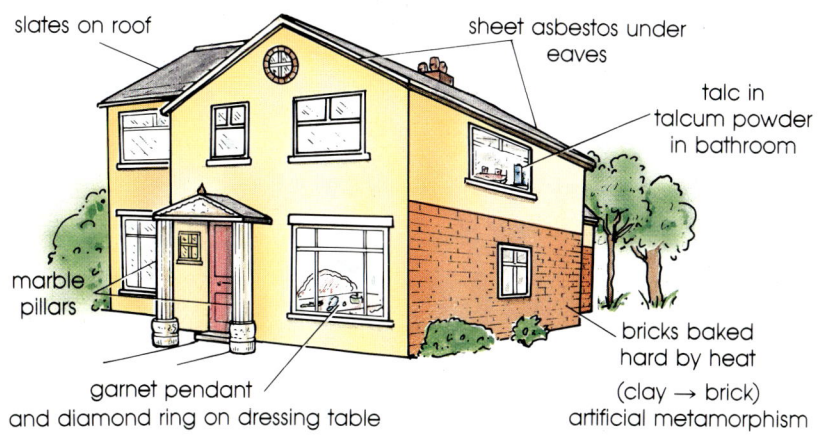

slates on roof

sheet asbestos under eaves

talc in talcum powder in bathroom

marble pillars

garnet pendant and diamond ring on dressing table

bricks baked hard by heat

(clay → brick) artificial metamorphism

C The metamorphic mansion.

Now try these

1 What does the word 'metamorphism' mean?

2 What changes would need to happen for carbon in a biscuit to become a diamond?

3 What are the two main forces which cause metamorphism?

4 Which of these two forces was involved in the baking of the cake?

5 Look at Fig c. Make a list of all the metamorphic rocks and minerals shown in the diagram. Which metamorphic material was formed by the same process as Lotti's cake?

6 What does heat and pressure actually do to a rock?

7 Where does the heat and pressure come from?

8 Complete the following **WP** passage, filling in the missing words chosen from the ones below:

pressure; roofing; mineral; cloth; sheets; insulation; suits; uses; powder; machine; rings; heat.

Slate is formed by _____ metamorphism. It is widely used as a _____ material. Fibrous asbestos is a metamorphic _____. It can be made into _____ or pressed into _____. It is an excellent _____ and firemen's _____ are made from it. Talc has two main _____. It is made into talcum powder, and is used as a machine lubricant. The metamorphic minerals diamond and _____ are used as ornaments in _____ and pendants. Clay is changed by _____ into hard bricks.

39

ROCKS AND WEATHERING

2.10 Uses of rocks

What are the important uses for rocks? Did you know that your pet probably eats rocks every day? Why? Limestone is added to pet food. The calcium in it is good for bones and teeth.

Try this

Think of all the ways rocks are used in everyday life, and make a list of them. At the end of this unit look at your list again and add any missing items.

Building stone

Granite and limestone are the most important rocks used for building stone. Sandstone, slate and marble are also used. Blocks of building stone have to be free of cracks and carefully split away from the rock face in a quarry. This means stone is usually more expensive than other building materials.

Quarried stone

Most of the stone in the UK is quarried. In the quarry the rock is usually blasted off the rock face by explosives. Then it is crushed into small pieces or powdered. The table opposite shows the main uses for quarried stone.

Granite and limestone are hard rocks and they both make excellent roadstone. Chippings of rock are mixed with tar to make asphalt. This is rolled flat to make the road's top layer.

A The Taj Mahal: a building made of marble.

Uses of quarried stone	
roadstone	48%
concrete	24%
iron/steel, fertilisers and animal feed	16%
building blocks	8%
rail track ballast	4%

Do you know what different kinds of rock are used for? Here is a list of five rocks: clay; marble; slate; limestone; granite. Spider diagrams showing their uses have been drawn in Fig b for each rock, but the rock's name has been left out of each one. Can you decide what they should be? Copy the five diagrams and write in the names of the rocks.

Activity 2.15

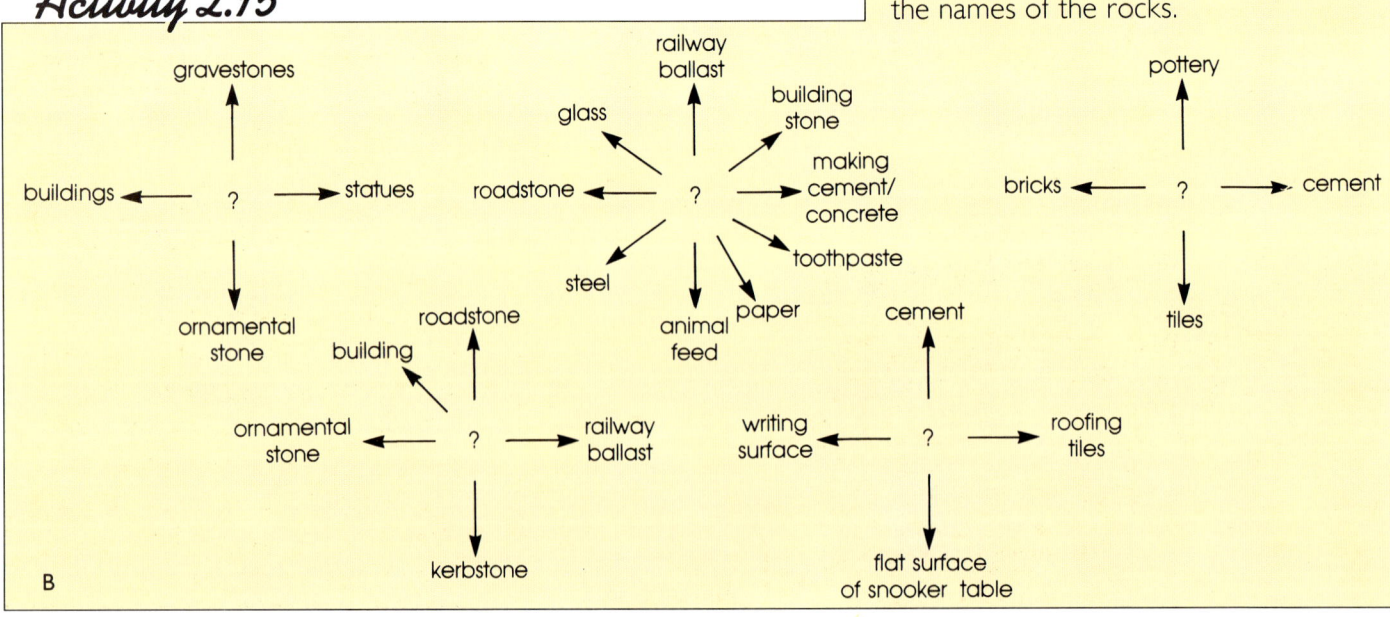

Artificial stone

The most familiar building materials are mortar, concrete and bricks. Although these are artificial, they come from rocks.

Mortar is the mixture used to hold bricks together in a wall. It is made by mixing sand and cement.

Concrete also uses natural stone. Crushed rock (chippings) and sand are mixed with cement. Even the cement comes from heated limestone powder mixed with clay. The advantage of concrete is that it can be poured into moulds. Once it sets it is as strong as ordinary rock and in exactly the required shape. Concrete has many uses: paving stone and pipes are made from it as well as bridges and high office blocks.

D What is cement made of?

Activity 2.16

Making concrete

Mix cupfuls of gravel (chippings), sand and cement together on a flat surface covered with thick polythene. When thoroughly mixed, make a hollow in the top of the mound, and add some water. Let the water soak in, then mix thoroughly. Be careful not to add too much water and make the mix too sloppy. Pour the concrete into a prepared shape. This could be a wooden box or simply a plastic cup. Leave it to set for at least a day. Later, test the hardened concrete to see how hard and strong it is. (Can you scratch it easily with a nail or your fingernail? Can you break pieces off?)

If the amounts of the ingredients are different, is the concrete stronger or weaker? Here are three different mixtures, but you could test other combinations:

Gravel	Sand	Cement
5 parts	3 parts	1 part
1 part	3 parts	5 parts
1 part	1 part	1 part

C Laying concrete pipes.

Now try these

1 Why is limestone added to pet food?
2 Which of the five kinds of rock shown in the spider diagrams has the most uses?
3 Name the two most important rocks used for building stone.
4 Below is a list of reasons why these two rocks are important. Copy the list of reasons in order of importance:
both rocks have a good colour and texture; they are easily available in many parts of the country; they are hard; they are easy to quarry in blocks; they are strong; there are few cracks in each block.
5 Look at the table showing the uses of quarried stone and make a pie chart or bar chart of the information.
6 Contact a local working (DTP) quarry for a visit and take photographs of (or sketch) the different stages in the quarrying process. Write an account of what happens. In your report, also answer the following questions: Do you think quarries make a mess of the countryside? Should it be stopped? Where would we get the stone from if it was stopped?

ROCKS AND WEATHERING

2.11 Uses of minerals and ores

Can you imagine what it would be like if we could not use minerals? There would be no metals at all because they all come from minerals.

Try this

> Make a list of all the objects you can think of in and around your home that are made of metal or come from minerals.

Now let's eavesdrop on the children. . .

'Just think what would happen if all metal and minerals suddenly vanished,' said Tom.

'It would be a mess in the kitchen cupboard,' said Liz. 'It's full of baked beans and soup!'

'How could I eat my dinner if there were no knives and forks?' said Lotti.

'You would have to learn to use chopsticks,' said Tom.

'Or use your fingers!' said Liz.

'Just think,' said Tom. 'We wouldn't be able to lock the door at night — the key and the lock wouldn't be there.'

'This is silly,' said Liz. 'I'm off to buy an ice-cream.'

'You can't,' said Lotti. 'All the coins in your purse have vanished!'

This is what it said in Lotti's book on 'Minerals'. . .

Activity 2.17

Some other metals and their uses

(WP) In this table, the 'uses' have become jumbled up. Try to rewrite the table and get the 'uses' in the correct positions.

Main ore	Metal	Use (jumbled up)
bauxite	aluminium	layering on steel food cans; solder
malachite	copper	paints; petrol; solder
gold	gold	strong, lightweight metal
galena	lead	conducts electricity, made into wires and cables
cassiterite	tin	rare, valuable, used in jewellery

Diamond
This is the world's hardest natural material. Small pieces of diamonds are embedded on metal drilling bits and on saw blades so that they can cut through hard rocks more easily. 'Rough' diamonds can also be cut to make beautiful jewellery.

Metal ores
Any mineral which contains a useful metal worth extracting is called an **ore**. Iron and steel are used to make all kinds of products — from cars and washing machines to knives and forks. Haematite (Fig c) is one of the main iron ores. To extract the metal, the ore is mixed with limestone and coke (from coal). It is then heated in a furnace to 1500°C. Chemical reactions take place and iron is formed. Then the molten metal is poured off.

A The uses of aluminium. How many can you spot?

Activity 2.18

Some other minerals and their uses

(WP) Again, the 'uses' in the table are jumbled. Try to sort them out.

Mineral	Use (jumbled up)
asbestos	talcum powder and toothpaste
halite	soft carbon, mixed with clay to make 'lead' pencils
graphite	
quartz	for bricks and pottery
clay	sapphire, ruby, opal, jade and emerald are all highly valued jewellery stones
gemstones	
talc	common salt for flavouring food
	artificial version used in electronics, eg watches; sandpaper
	to insulate in fireproof materials

Using clay

Clay has been used for hundreds of years to make bricks for building. In hot, dry climates it is possible to leave clay bricks out in the sun to bake dry. Then they can be used for building. When bricks are used in cooler, wetter climates, the bricks need to be much harder. They are heated and baked in kilns or ovens to make them hard.

Activity 2.19

Using clay to make bricks

Roll out some moistened potter's clay – enough to make a block about 20 cm long by 3 cm wide and 1 cm thick. Divide the block into four 'bricks'. Seal one brick in a plastic bag. Leave two of the bricks on top of a warm radiator to dry. Put the fourth brick into an oven at a setting of 150°C. When the radiator bricks have dried out, arrange to have one of the bricks 'fired' in a kiln. (This should only be done by an expert and your Art Department may be able to help.)

After two days compare the four bricks.

1 Which dried out the fastest/slowest?
2 What colour was each brick?
3 Which was the hardest? (Scratch with a nail or your fingernail.)
4 Which was the strongest? (Can you break pieces off?)
5 What was the purpose of the brick in the plastic bag?
6 Which of the bricks would be best to use for building purposes? Say why.

B Bauxite: the only mineral ore of aluminium.

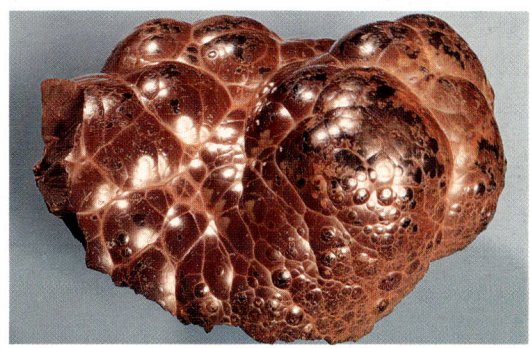

C Haematite: a rich iron-ore mineral.

Now try these

1 How many home objects did you list at the beginning of this unit that were made of metal or minerals?
2 Why are saws and drills studded with diamonds?
3 If diamonds themselves have to be cut, how do you suppose this might be done?
4 What is the name given to any mineral containing metal that is worth extracting?
5 Fill in the missing words in **(WP)** this passage using the ones listed below.

pure; reacts; coke; haematite; furnaces; ores; temperature.

_____ is one of the iron _____. It is reacted in big _____. The limestone _____ with impurities and the _____ burns to give _____ of 1500°C. When the iron melts, the _____ metal is poured off.

6 'Brick is an artificial metamorphic rock.' Try to explain what this sentence means. (Look back to Unit 2.9).

TECTONIC PROCESSES

3.1 Changes in rock layers 2

Why are some rocks folded instead of being in flat layers? What are upfolds and downfolds? How can flat layers of rock become mountain ranges?

Lotti, Liz and Tom decided to cycle back to the disused railway cutting they had seen the day before to do some more exploring. As they rode along the path they noticed something rather strange — the layers of rock were no longer flat but slanting. Further on the rock layers rose and fell in huge folds (see Fig a below). Tom started to daydream. He found himself on a Big Dipper — going slowly up to the crest of each fold, then rushing steeply to the trough. . .

A Tom's Big Dipper 'rock ride'.

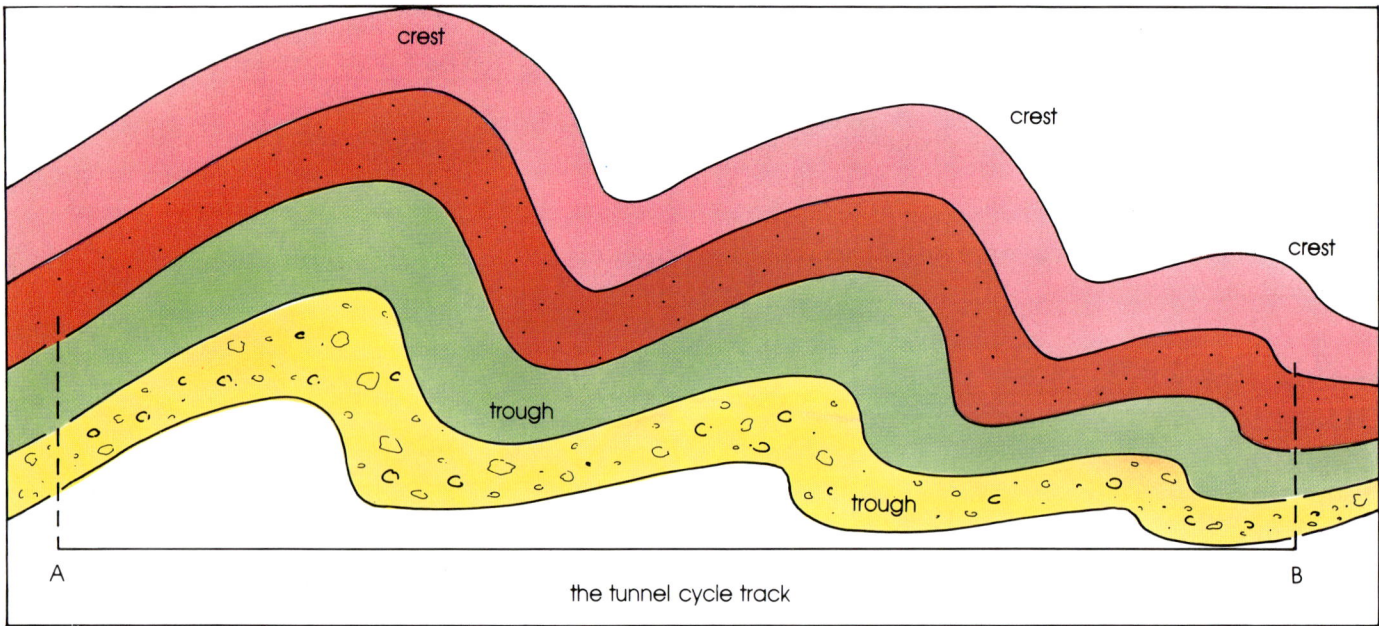

'Our tablecloth is like this,' said Lotti.

'What do you mean?' said Liz.

'Well, if you push the cloth on the table top it goes into folds,' said Lotti.

'But rocks aren't soft like a tablecloth, I wonder how it could happen?' said Liz.

'If the layers were squeezed flat again,' said Lotti, 'then they would take up more space.'

'Don't do that,' said Tom. 'You could ruin the ride!' The girls looked at him oddly.

Activity 3.1

Divide into pairs or small groups. Together write a statement answering questions 1, 2 and 3 below – to be read out later to the rest of the class.

1 If rocks are hard, then how could they be pushed into folds?
2 What force could do this?
3 Using a tape measure and some string, Liz was able to work out how much more space the rocks once occupied. Look at the diagram of the rocks in the railway cutting at the top of the page and see if you can do the same. Your answer should be in metres.

B Rocks are pushed into huge folds to make mountain ranges: Stair hole, Dorset.

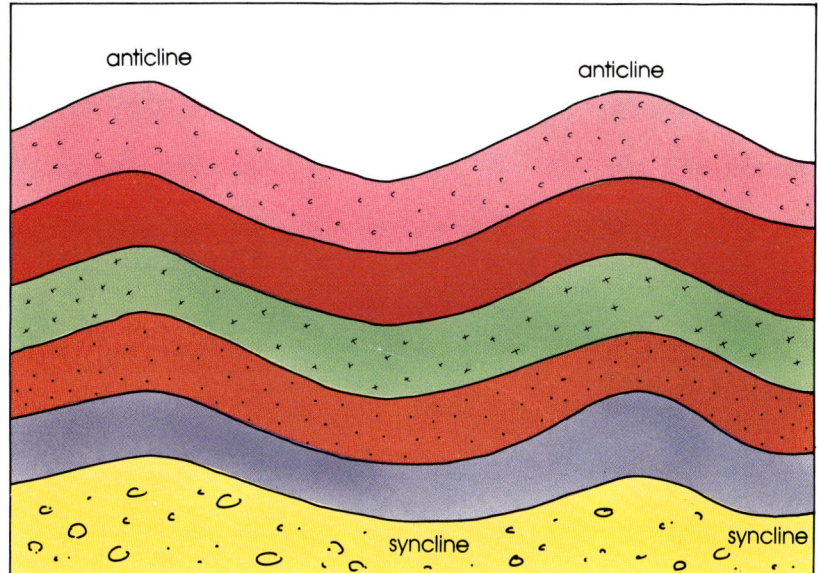

C Anticlines and synclines.

Activity 3.2

Making folds

Try to think of a way of making folds using different coloured Plasticine.

1 Begin by building up flat layers of Plasticine.
2 Then imitate pressures in the Earth by pushing the layers with two blocks of wood (Fig d).
3 Make a sketch of the folds you have produced.
4 Label the anticlines and synclines.

Now try these

1 What is the height of Mount Everest in kilometres?
2 Name two examples of fold mountain ranges.
3 What are other names for the 'crests' and 'troughs' on Tom's 'Big Dipper' (Fig a)?
4 What evidence is there that the rocks at the summit of Mount Everest were once on the sea bed?
5 How many anticlines and synclines can you see in the photograph in Fig b?
6 Complete the word puzzle in Fig e to find the name of the mystery mountains, using these clues:
  1 Rock layers before folding.
  2 A downfold.
  3 Curved structures in rock layers.
  4 Found near the summit of Mount Everest.
  5 The top of a fold.
7 Using an atlas world map (physical), find out where the main fold mountain ranges are. Mark them on an outline map of the world.

This is what it said about folds in Lotti's book:

What are folds?

Layers of rock become folded when they are put under a lot of sideways pressure. The rocks are pushed into a smaller amount of space and they crumple upwards. The upfold is called an **anticline** and the downfold is called a **syncline** (Fig c). Mountain ranges like the Alps in Europe and the Himalayas in Asia are made of huge folds (Fig b). The highest mountain in the world is Mount Everest. The folded rock layers near its summit contain fossil sea shells that were once flat on the sea floor. Now they are 8848 metres above sea level.

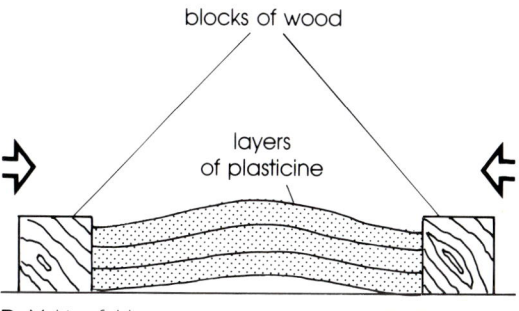

D Making folds.

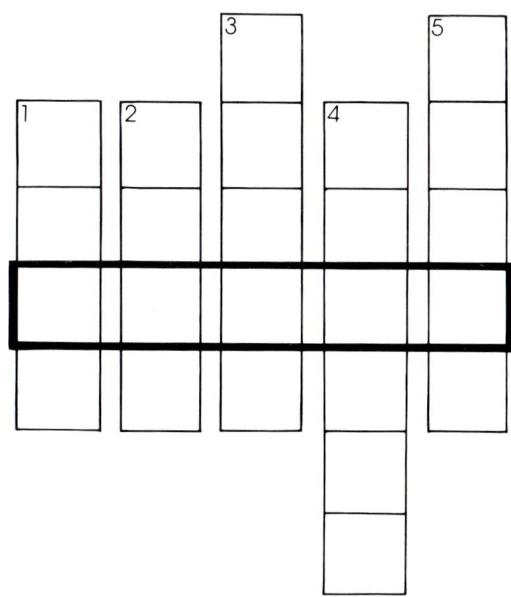

E

45

TECTONIC PROCESSES

3.2 Volcanoes

Lotti, Liz and Tom were looking at a book on 'Volcanoes'. 'I know,' said Liz. 'Let's write down all the questions about volcanoes we can think of!'

'That's a great idea,' said Tom.

'After that we can read the book and try to find the answers,' said Lotti. Here are the questions the children thought of:

Try this

- Read through the questions below and talk about them. Then write down the answers to any questions you think you know.
- Also write down three questions of your own.
1 What is the usual shape of most volcanoes?
2 Is it true that volcanoes 'smoke'?
3 Do volcanoes produce ash?
4 How many active volcanoes are there?
5 How many volcanoes erupt each year?
6 Do volcanoes have ice and snow on their summits?
7 Is it true that volcanoes produce 'bombs'?
8 Do volcanoes ever explode?
9 If volcanoes are so dangerous why do people live on them?
10 Can gases from volcanoes kill people?
11 What is 'magma' and 'lava'?
12 What makes a volcano erupt?

This is what the book on 'Volcanoes' said:

A volcano is usually a cone-shaped mountain (see Fig a). Volcanoes allow hot, molten rock called **magma** from inside the Earth to escape. This happens in an eruption. **Lava** is the name given to magma which has reached the surface (Fig b). Apart from lava, volcanoes erupt hot gases and ash. Ash is made of powdered rock and lava droplets. Huge explosions in a volcano blast out the ash with tremendous force. Ash clouds mixed with water vapour can make people think volcanoes 'smoke'. In fact there is no fire. The ash is not produced by burning. However, if hot lava, with a temperature of 1000°C, touches trees, they will be set alight.

A Volcanoes are usually cone-shaped.

B The top of a lava flow.

What happens in an eruption?

In many volcanoes, an eruption begins with violent explosions. Hot gases are held at very high pressures in the magma beneath the volcano. These pressures build up because the central **pipe** and **vent** are blocked by old, hard lava (Fig c). Just before an eruption a volcano will swell slightly as the gases and the magma push upwards. Eventually the blockage in the vent is cleared by an explosion. Sometimes the explosion is so powerful that the top part of the volcano can be blasted away. Can you see where this happened near the top of the volcano shown in Fig c?

In the Mount St Helens eruption in 1980 (Fig d) the whole of one side of the volcano exploded. There was a huge sideways blast of ash — enough to flatten trees and kill people several kilometres away.

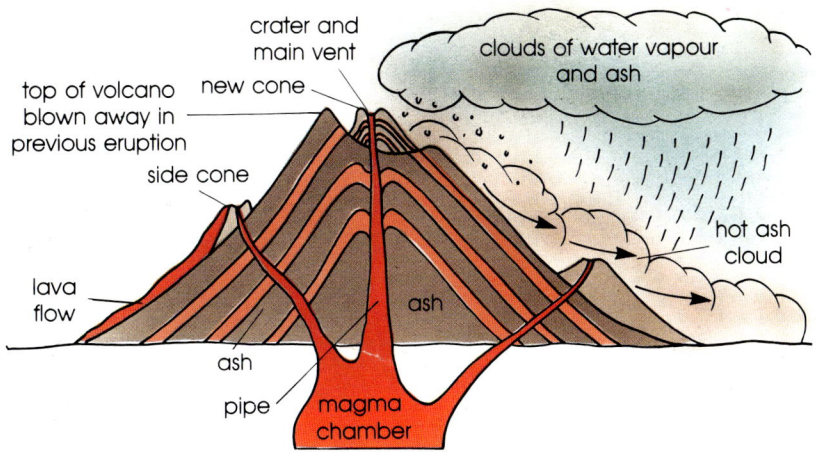

C The structure of a volcano.

Structure of a volcano

Fig c shows the structure of a typical volcano. You will see that the sides are made of layers of ash and lava, erupted at different times. Each eruption must have begun explosively with ash being produced, followed later by lava. Look carefully at the diagram – how many separate eruptions can you count?

Where are the world's volcanoes?

Most of the world's active volcanoes are found in long, narrow belts. Many of them are in a ring surrounding the Pacific Ocean. This is sometimes called the 'Ring of Fire' (see Fig e).

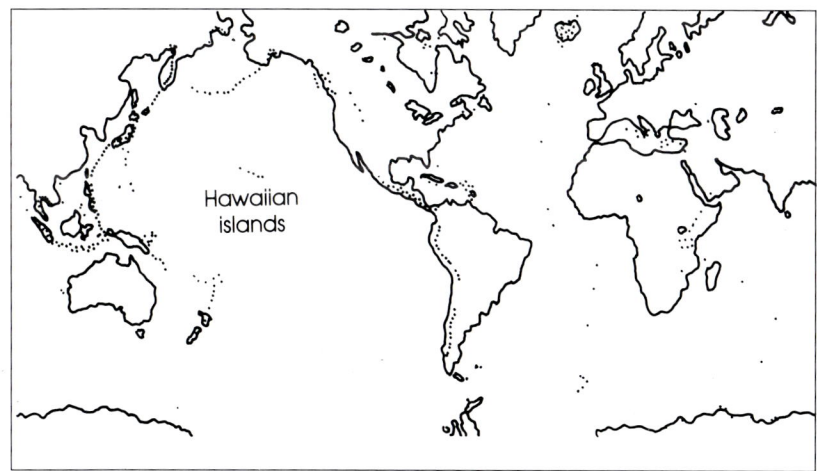

E The world's volcanoes. Each dot stands for a volcano which has erupted in historic time.

How do volcanoes kill people?

The explosions in a volcano can throw blobs of lava many hundreds of metres into the air. These are called **bombs**. Recently a volcano in Japan began throwing out bombs. Three tourists died as the hot rocks rained down.

D Mt St Helens exploded in a huge ash eruption in 1980. 60 people were killed.

Ash eruptions are dangerous because people can either choke to death or be buried alive. Poisonous gases such as carbon monoxide have also killed many people. One recent disaster was the 1985 eruption of Nevada del Ruiz in Columbia. The heat from the volcano melted snow and ice. A huge river of mud flowed down into the valley below. The town of Armero was buried and 23 000 people were killed.

Why live near a volcano?

It may seem strange that people live so near to danger. However, most people who live on the slopes of a volcano never see an eruption. Also the soil on the slopes of many volcanoes is good for growing crops because of the dissolved minerals from ancient ash deposits. Many islands, large and small, are almost entirely made of volcanoes, eg Java and Japan. It would not make sense to get everyone to leave their homes just on the chance of an eruption happening once in every few hundred years.

Now try these

1 Write down the answers to the questions at the start of this unit.
2 Make up headlines and (DTP) newspaper stories to fill a front page, reporting on an eruption.
3 Make a list of the different ways volcanoes can cause loss of life.

TECTONIC PROCESSES

3.3 Volcanic islands

Can volcanoes ever form new land? What happens when sea water mixes with magma? What is the link between volcanoes and coral islands? Can rocks float in water?

Liz met Tom and Lotti after school. 'I've got some real problems here,' she said. 'Can you two help me? Just look at these science homework questions!'

'Ugh! They look really awkward,' said Lotti. 'Where can we find the answers?'

'I know!' said Tom. 'Let's look them up in my encyclopaedia.'

This is what they found out:

A new island: Surtsey

In November 1963, a fisherman to the south of Iceland noticed dead fish floating round his boat. He looked over the side and was amazed to see a dull red glow − the sea was steaming and hot! A few days later a new volcano/island appeared. At first it just erupted ash and lava bombs. Sea water poured into the crater and mixed with the magma. There were violent explosions. As the cone grew, the crater was raised above sea level. Then the volcano began to erupt lava.

Today Surtsey island covers an area of nearly three square kilometres and the top is 170 metres above sea level (see Fig a). It has not erupted since 1965.

Krakatoa: an island explodes

Krakatoa was a volcanic island between the larger islands of Java and Sumatra. In 1883 the island was destroyed by a huge explosion (Fig b). The noise was heard 5000 kilometres away. Most of the island was blown 80 kilometres into the sky. Huge amounts of ash spread out through the atmosphere, and the world had a series of cool summers and freezing winters. The explosion disturbed the sea, making giant sea waves, called **tsunami**. Such waves are more often produced by earthquakes. The giant waves swept along the coastline of Java and Sumatra, drowning 36 000 people.

Pumice

In both the Surtsey and the Krakatoa eruptions, people reported seeing large masses of floating **pumice**. Pumice is a light and frothy lava, full of gas bubbles.

A New land appears: Surtsey Island.

Before the explosion

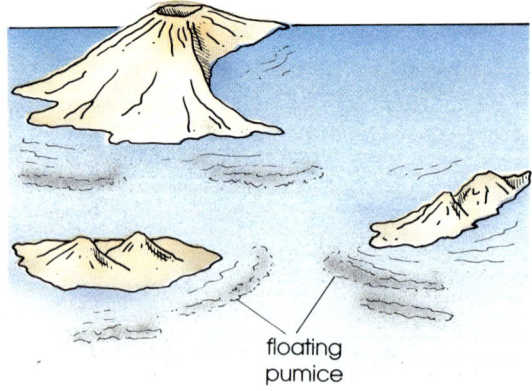

After the explosion − note the two smaller islands are bigger because of the addition of ash.

B Krakatoa.

Coral islands

In warm, tropical seas are thousands of coral islands called **atolls**. These islands are made entirely of coral. There is no rock. Corals grow in warm, shallow water, usually to depths of about 30 metres. The puzzle is that in many atolls, coral reefs are found to depths of over 1000 metres. How could the coral begin growing at such a depth? One idea to explain this mystery is that coral growth began on the shores of a volcano (see Fig c). As time passes, the sea level rises. The island volcano is drowned but the coral animals keep pace and continue to build up their reefs. Deep holes drilled into atolls have found lava from old volcanoes, so this seems to be true.

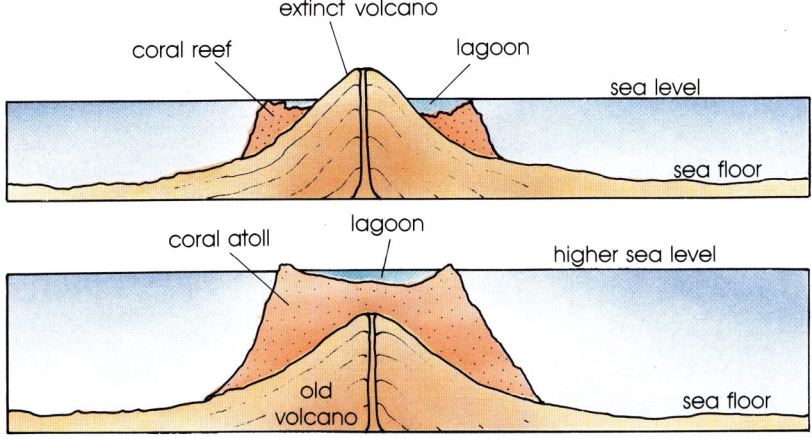

C How a coral atoll forms.

Volcanoes and British scenery

There are no active volcanoes in the British Isles today, but plenty of dead ones like the Edinburgh volcano (see Unit 2.4). This volcano was active 350 million years ago. Then, 290 million years ago, there was a huge mass of magma called a **bathylith** pushing its way beneath the rock layers of south-west England (Fig d). It cooled and became solid granite. The moors of Bodmin in Cornwall and Dartmoor in Devon were formed in this way. The granite is now found at the surface because erosion has worn away most of the sedimentary rocks that covered it. The Isles of Scilly are made entirely of granite.

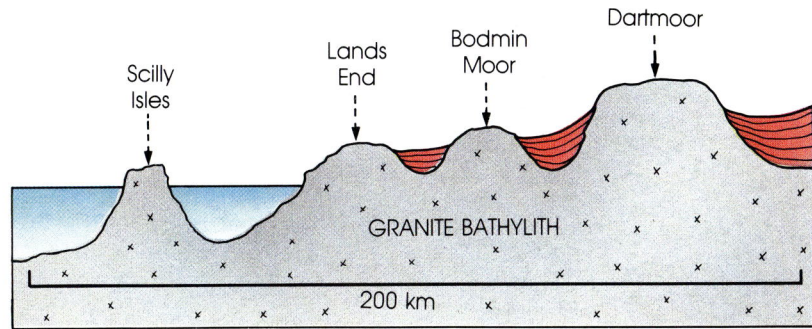

D The bathylith of SW England.

Activity 3.3

Looking at volcanic products

Pumice

Examine a sample of pumice (Fig e). Can you see the gas bubble holes? How do you think this rock formed? What happens if you drop it in water?

E Pumice: once a frothy lava.

Ash

Look at a sample of volcanic ash in a sealed jar. Shake the jar — how long does it take to settle? Shake the jar again, then remove the jar cover for a few seconds. What happens?

Volcanic tuff

This sample is a rock formed from layers of ash which have been pressed down to form a hard rock. Can you see any layers? Look carefully at the tiny ash grains using a hand lens.

Now try these

1 Answer the four questions at the start of this unit.
2 Explain how Krakatoa caused a change in the world's climate. Do you think the change was a long-lasting one? Give reasons.
3 What are the two ways in which giant sea waves called tsunami are made?
4 Why does pumice float?
5 Explain how atolls form.
6 How has underground magma affected the scenery of SW England?

TECTONIC PROCESSES

3.4 Earthquakes

Lotti was reading the newspaper. Tom and Liz were playing cards. 'Come on Lotti — it can't be that interesting,' said Liz. 'What's it about?'

'What can kill 100 000 people and flatten a city?' asked Lotti.

'Bombs?' answered Tom.

'A nuclear power station blowing up?' asked Liz.

'No,' said Lotti, 'you're both wrong — a natural event so powerful that no one can stop it. Have another guess. . .'

This is what Lotti was reading about:

A A building tilts at a crazy angle in the wrecked town of Spitak.

Friday December 9 1988

The Daily Post

THOUSANDS KILLED

ON WEDNESDAY, up to 100 000 people were killed by an earthquake in Soviet Armenia. Countless dead and injured lie beneath tonnes of rubble. Schools, hospitals and thousands of homes have been flattened. The town of Spitak, once home to 30 000 people, was reduced to a pile of rubble. It is so badly damaged that it will never be rebuilt in the same place. Children were in their classrooms when the earthquake struck. In Spitak only one of the eight schools was left standing. Soldiers were pulling the bodies of hundreds of children from the rubble. Such was the power of the quake that it ripped up 24 miles of railway track. Bridges and electricity cables were brought down. Many roads are badly damaged — the road surfaces were smashed into sections and are lying at crazy angles.

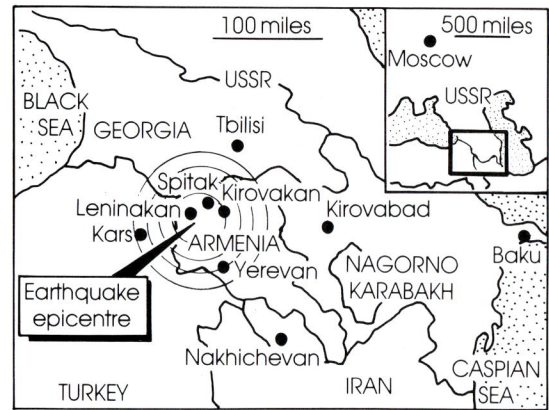

B Map of the Armenian earthquake. Which three cities would have suffered the most damage?

What is an earthquake?

The Armenian earthquake struck at 10.41 a.m. on Wednesday December 7, 1988. It was caused by two 60-second quakes, five minutes apart. In all big earthquakes the ground shakes violently, caused by a sudden release of energy in the rocks below. As the rocks 'break' there is a sudden movement. The point where the rocks break is called the **focus** (see Fig d). This may be quite near the surface or up to 700 kilometres underground. In the Armenian earthquake it was just 25 kilometres beneath the surface — this was one reason why the earthquake was so destructive. The vibrations or shock waves travel away from the focus in all directions. The nearest point on the surface to the focus is called the **epicentre**. This is where there will be the most damage (see Fig b).

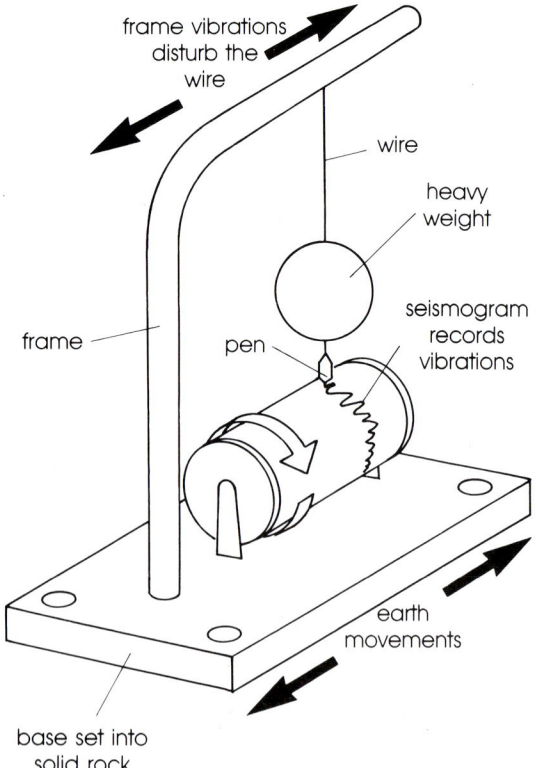

C A seismometer.

How can an earthquake be measured?

The instrument used to measure earthquakes is called a **seismometer** (Fig c). Seismometers are very sensitive and can detect tiny movements of as little as a thousandth of a millimetre. For example, the Armenian earthquake was picked up by a seismometer in Edinburgh, more than 2000 miles from the epicentre. In fact the instruments are so sensitive that scientists have to be careful about where they put them – well away from railways and motorways.

Earthquakes used to be detected by standing rods of varying lengths and thicknesses on end. The thickest, shortest rods only fell down if the earthquake was really severe. You can try this too.

Another way of measuring earthquakes is to observe the amount of damage caused (see Fig e). The 12-point Mercalli scale was devised by G Mercalli in 1902. Nowadays seismometers use the Richter scale. This was devised by Charles Richter in 1935. The energy released by a big earthquake (8.6 Richter) is about the same as the energy released by a 100-megaton nuclear explosion — that is 5000 times the power of the bomb that destroyed the Japanese city of Hiroshima at the end of the Second World War.

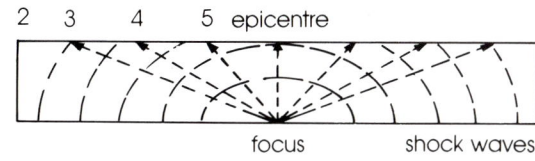

D The damage is greatest at the epicentre and least at 2.

MERCALLI Intensity (degree of shaking)	Description of characteristic effects	RICHTER Magnitude (total energy released)
I	Instrumental: detected only by seismographs	2
II	Feeble: felt only by sensitive people	3
III	Slight: like the vibrations due to a passing light lorry	
IV	Moderate: like the passing of a heavy road vehicle; rocking of loose objects, including standing cars	4
V	Rather strong: felt by most people; church bells ring	5
VI	Most people frightened; windows broken; dishes fall out of cupboards	
VII	Very strong; general alarm; walls crack; plaster falls	
VIII	Destructive: car drivers find it difficult to steer; masonry cracked; chimneys fall	6
IX	Ruinous: general panic; ground cracks appear and pipes break open	
X	Disastrous: ground cracks badly; many buildings destroyed; landslides on steep slopes	7
XI	Very disastrous: most buildings and bridges destroyed; all services (railways, pipes and cables) out of action; great landslides and floods; dams badly damaged	
XII	Catastrophic: total destruction; objects thrown into air; ground rises and falls in waves; cracks open and close	8

E Measuring earthquakes.

Activity 3.4

Making a seismometer
Choose 10 pieces of wooden dowel rod of different lengths and thicknesses. Your thinnest rods should be about the diameter of a pencil, down to a thicker rod about the size of a cotton reel. Stand the rods upright on one end of a table. Space out the rods to avoid the 'domino effect' of them knocking each other over. Then bang the top of the table at the other end. How many rods fall over? Which person in your group can produce the biggest 'earthquake'? How can you tell which was the biggest 'earthquake'?

Now try these

1 From what you have read of the Armenian disaster, what point do you think it reached on the Mercalli scale?

2 The following reports of earthquakes also appeared in the newspapers at the same time as the Armenian disaster. In each case decide the value on the Mercalli scale:

   a 'An earth tremor shook doors, windows and plates in cup- boards in East Anglia yesterday.'

   b 'An earthquake shook a region near Naples in Italy on Wednesday night. People were woken up and some windows were broken.'

SOIL

4.1 Looking at soil

Soil may not seem important, but without it there would be no food crops and millions of people would die!

Lotti and Liz were watching Tom digging his garden. He was getting out of breath. 'Why does it get harder to dig the deeper you go?' he sighed.

'I can think of one reason,' said Lotti. 'The deeper soil is heavier and it has more stones.'

'I can think of another reason,' said Liz. 'The top part of the soil is lighter and less waterlogged.'

'You are both brilliant!' said Tom. 'Now can you think of a reason why you can't help me?'

Have you ever helped with the gardening? If you have you'll know, like Tom, that digging can be very hard work. Usually the deeper you dig the harder it gets. Why is this?

Try this

1 There are many differences between the top layer **CP** (**topsoil**) and the lower layer (**subsoil**). Here is a list of statements about what soil is like:
   - easy to dig
   - hard to dig
   - many stones
   - few stones
   - fairly dark-coloured with plant remains
   - fairly light-coloured with no plant remains
   - in heavy clumps and waterlogged
   - light and crumbly
   - worms, ants or beetles present
   - no small animals present.

   Sort them out and decide which statements belong under these two headings: 'Subsoil – 50 cm depth', 'Topsoil (at surface)'.
2 If you continued to dig down, would the soil become stonier until eventually you reached solid rock?
3 Why do you think that soil layers are always at the surface on top of rocks? (See Fig a.)
4 Write the heading 'How does soil form from rocks?'. **WP** Look carefully at Fig a and write a short paragraph about what you think happens.
5 Plants grow in the topsoil because it is nearest the surface. Does this mean that the subsoil is no good for plant growth? Write down what you think, giving reasons.

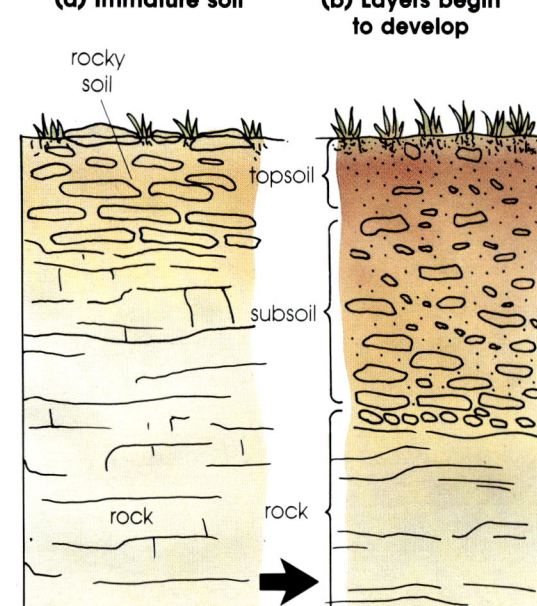

(a) Immature soil

rocky soil

rock

(b) Layers begin to develop

topsoil

subsoil

rock

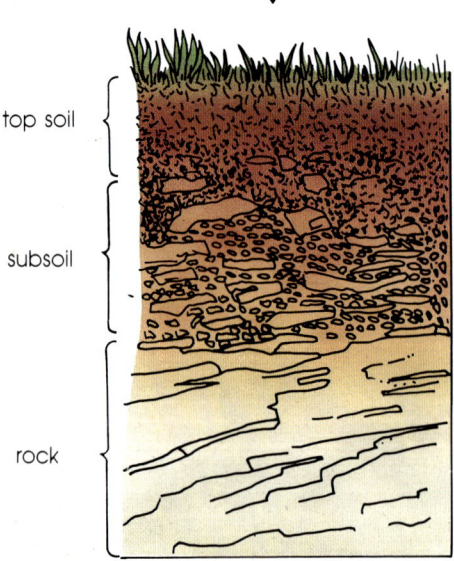

(c) Layers well developed

top soil

subsoil

rock

A How soil forms.

Where does soil come from?

Soil is made of rock fragments which have been broken down very slowly over many years. Rocks seem hard but they are softened and broken as they are attacked by frost and rain. This process is called **weathering**.

Rainwater can soak into rocks and soften and dissolve them (Fig b). Small cracks in the rocks can easily be widened by frost as ice expands. This helps to break rocks into fragments. Acids from plants such as lichens help to dissolve rocks (Fig c). Boulders, stones and pebbles are large fragments. They can be broken down even more to form gravel, sand and silt. The tiniest fragments of all are the clay particles.

C Lichens produce acid which helps to dissolve rocks and make soil.

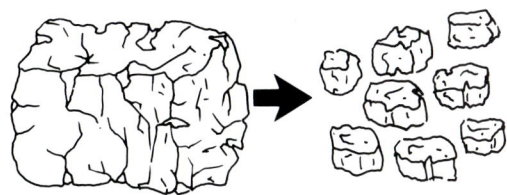

B Water seeps into cracks, softening the rock. Eventually it is broken into smaller fragments.

SOIL

4.2 What is in the soil?

Have you noticed how the topsoil layer is darker in colour than the subsoil? Why is this? What else does soil contain?

Tom and Lotti were digging a really deep trench. Tom said he was going to fill it up with compost and then plant beans. 'Beans love compost,' he said. 'It's so full of plant foods.'

'Ugh! It smells terrible — what is it?' said Liz.

'Don't you know?' said Tom. 'We put leaves, weeds and grass cuttings onto the compost heap. Then it all slowly rots and goes this black colour.'

'It's full of worms and things!' said Lotti.

'Yes,' said Tom. 'They eat it and help to break it down.'

'That explains why the topsoil is a darker colour,' said Lotti.

'I don't see how,' said Liz.

'Well read what it says in this garden book,' said Lotti. . .

A Tom's dad starts off his compost heap. What will it be like when it has rotted?

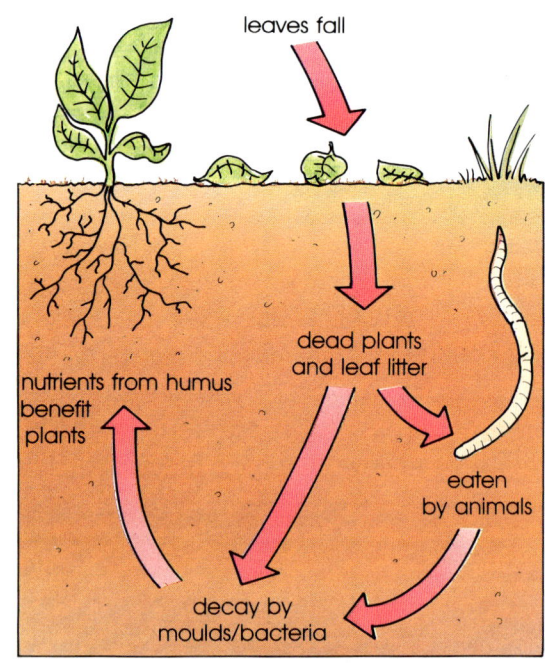

B The soil cycle.

In time, the remains of dead animals and plants left in the soil start to decay (see Fig b). Tiny bacteria and moulds feed on the remains. They break it down into fragments. The decaying matter left in the soil is called **humus**. It mixes with the mineral fragments from rocks to give a crumbly structure. The dark-coloured humus is very good for the soil. It improves soil structure and releases plant foods called **nutrients**. These make the soil fertile and good for plants to grow in.

What animals do to the soil

Animals like earthworms, slugs and millipedes also feed on humus. The activity of soil animals is very good for the soil. Earthworm burrows allow air and water to enter the soil. This is important for the growth of plant roots. Earthworms eat soil and break it down into finer particles. This releases even more nutrients for plants. If the soil is healthy, there are about 37 earthworms in every square metre. In one year they will bring about 3 kilograms of fine soil to the surface as worm casts.

What else is there in soil?

So far, you have found that soil contains mineral particles from rocks, living plants and animals, and humus. What else does soil contain?

Activity 4.3

1 Why is the topsoil darker than the subsoil?
2 What part do animals play in the soil-making process?
3 Why is there a 'cycle' in the soil? What is being moved through the cycle? (See Fig b.) Write down your conclusions.

Activity 4.4

Put a sample of soil in a beaker with a watchglass on top. Heat the soil gently (Fig c). Write down what you see happening. What does this tell you about another ingredient of soil?

Activity 4.5

Does the soil contain air?

Fill a measuring cylinder with soil, up to 50 millilitres. Fill a second measuring cylinder with water up to the same mark. Then pour the water into the first cylinder (Fig d). Watch what happens as the water soaks into the soil.

1 Write down what you saw.
2 Write down the final level of soil and water mixture. Was it 100 millilitres? If not, explain why.
3 What does this activity show about what soil must contain? Write down your conclusions.

Now try these

1 What is compost? Why do gardeners add it to the soil?
2 What is humus? How does it form?
3 What is meant by a 'nutrient'? Where do nutrients come from and what good do they do in the soil?
4 Explain how soil animals improve soil quality.
5 What are the five main ingredients of soil?
6 Apart from nutrients, name two other substances that plant roots need for healthy growth.
7 Complete the word puzzle (Fig e) using these clues:
   1 Makes topsoil fertile.
   2 Makes soil darker.
   3 Lower part of a plant.
   4 A soil animal.
   5 Tom makes this.
   6 Another word for 'decay'.
   7 Cuttings of this make good compost.
   8 Another word for 'pile'.
   9 A precise position.
   10 (across) Holes that worms make.
   10 (down) This can ache with too much digging.
   11 The darker soil layer is this.
   12 Worms make these on the surface.
   13 To blend.
8 Make your own compost heap and find out how long it takes for plant remains to form humus.
9 Talk to any neighbours you know who are gardeners. How many of them have compost heaps?

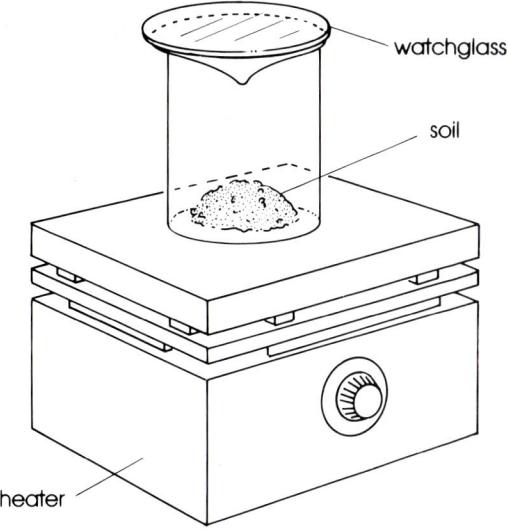

C Heating a soil sample.

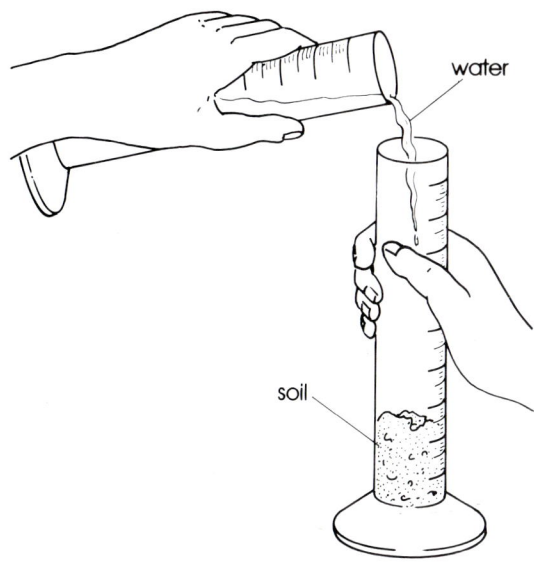

D What does this show?

E

SOIL

4.3 Soil texture

Did you know that the size of the rock grains in a soil can affect how well plants grow? This is called **soil texture**.

Try this

Lotti's garden has a clay soil. Tom's garden has a sandy soil. Liz's garden has a soil somewhere in between a clay and a sand soil. Also, Liz's garden has had a lot of compost added to it to improve it. Try to sort out which report belongs to each garden.

Report A
'My soil is light and easy to dig. It never gets flooded however hard it rains, so the drainage is good. There is a problem in dry weather because it dries out quickly. The rain washes a lot of plant foods downwards so we have to add extra plant foods.'

Report B
'My soil is heavy and hard to dig. When it rains a lot, it gets flooded, so the drainage is poor. In a dry spell, big cracks appear and it goes really hard, like concrete.'

Report C
'My soil is crumbly and full of plant roots and leaves. It drains well but does not dry out too much in a spell of dry weather. Plants do really well in it.'

Could you sort the reports out? If not, then these notes will help you. . .

Nearly all of the features mentioned in the three reports are caused by the soil texture. Fig a shows a microscopic view of **sand** and **clay** soils. Notice how much bigger the soil grains are in the sand. This is a **coarse** texture. Clay and silt soils have a **fine** texture.

A coarse, sandy soil allows water to drain through it quickly. Very little water is stored by the soil, so it quickly dries out. Clay and silt soils are so fine that water has difficulty passing between the grains, so these soils easily become waterlogged.

Do you remember Liz's garden? It was a mixture of sand, clay and silt. This soil texture is called a **loam**. A loam is the best texture for growing crops. It can be worked easily and is neither too wet nor too dry.

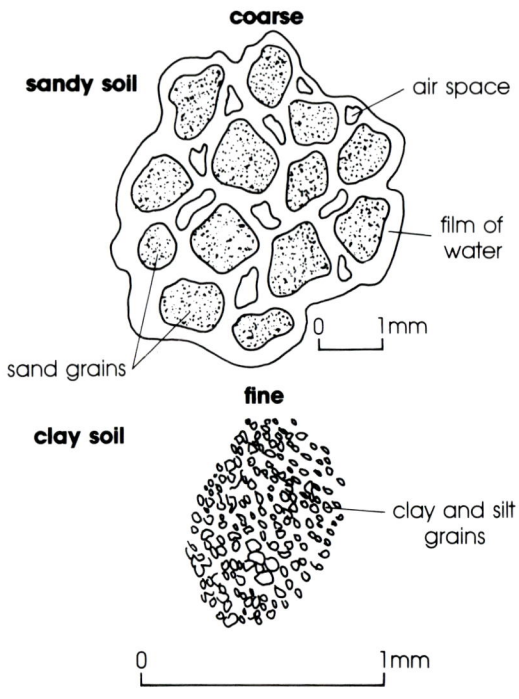

A Soil texture: sand and clay.

Activity 4.6

Comparing soil textures

Soil texture can be tested easily by what a soil *feels* like. Sand feels gritty and rough, whereas clay and silt feel silky with sticky lumps. A loam has lumps which crumble easily to a smooth powder. Work in pairs.

1 Compare the 'dry' textures of a sand, clay and loam. Write down what you think each one feels like.

2 For each soil sample, put a small amount of soil in your hand and add water (see Fig b). Then work the soil into a moist ball. Now write down the 'wet' texture for each soil.

3 Compare your notes with other pairs. Are your opinions the same?

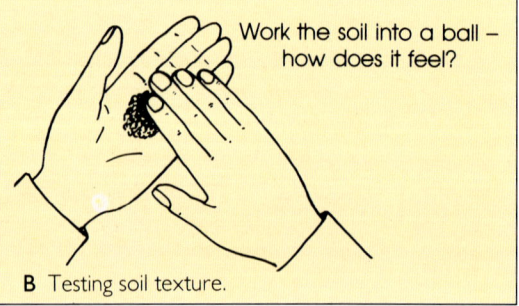

Work the soil into a ball – how does it feel?

B Testing soil texture.

Activity 4.7

The photographs, Figs c, d and e, show three soils.
1 Which is the sand/the clay/the loam?
2 Which soil is likely to have the highest humus content?

Activity 4.8

Comparing plant growth in sand, clay and loam

Work in pairs. Put each soil sample in a suitable container
(eg small plant pot), and dampen the soil. Then plant radish
seeds in each one (see Fig f). Keep the samples damp and
warm. (One pair could try giving their plants very little water
after they have sprouted.)

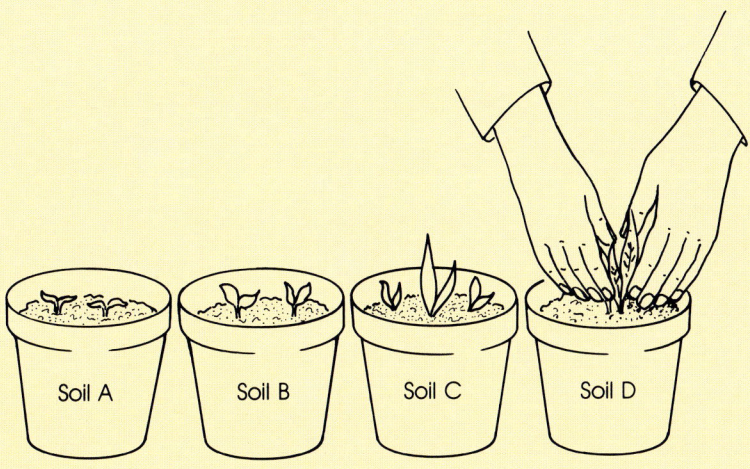

Soil A Soil B Soil C Soil D

F Comparing plant growth in different soils.

After the seeds begin to sprout, measure how fast they
grow over several days and keep a record, using a chart like
this:

	Height of seedlings in cm			
	Soil A	Soil B	Soil C	Soil D
Day 1				
Day 2				
Day 3				

1 Which soils produced the best/worst plant growth? Can
you think of reasons for this?
2 How did your results compare with other pairs?
3 Use the growth measurements to produce a simple **(CP)**
bar graph.

C Finely structured with loose grains: which soil is it?

D Forms sticky lumps: which soil is it?

E Well-structured and crumbly: which soil is it?

Now try these

1 Look at Fig a. Which soil texture
would have the most air spaces in
it?
2 The same diagram shows a sandy
(coarse) texture and a clay (fine)
texture. Make a sketch of what you
think a loam texture would be like.
3 Look back at the three reports of
Lotti's, Liz's and Tom's soils. Then
make a list of the good and bad
points of a clay and sandy soil,
under these headings:

Clay soil		Sandy soil	
Good points	Bad points	Good points	Bad points

4 Examine your own soil in your
garden at home and decide if it is a
sand, clay or loam. Write down
your reasons.

SOIL

4.4 Soil movement and soil types

Lotti's dad was worried (see Fig a). The garden wall was about to collapse. It was bulging outwards. Ever since the wet weather the problem had got worse.

Try this

1 Why do you think this was happening? Try to think of at least three reasons.
2 Write a short report to Lotti's dad explaining why **(WP)** and suggest ways he could stop it happening again.

This is what Lotti read in a book she found. Perhaps it will help you in your answers.

Soil often moves very slowly down a slope. This is called **soil creep**. Look carefully at Fig b below. Can you see the way the different soil types have slipped slowly down the slope? You will also see that different rock layers on the slope have produced different types of soil. An underlying rock which slowly weathers away to make a soil is called the **parent** rock.

Activity 4.9

1 Write down the name of each soil in Fig b and its parent rock.
2 Soil creep can cause other problems in the landscape. List at least three effects of soil creep that you can see in the diagram.
3 Why is the soil layer thin at the top of the slope and thick at the bottom? What force has caused this movement?

A Lotti's dad is worried.

Activity 4.10

Collecting soils from different rocks

Make a survey of the soils in your locality. You will need collecting bags with labels on them and a map. The best way to collect a soil sample is to use a soil auger. As you twist this into the soil it acts like a corkscrew. When you untwist it, the soil sample comes to the surface.

Each time you collect a soil sample, write a reference number on the bag and on the map. Also note the kind of place, eg your garden, a wood, a sandy place, a clay bank.

You will find that your samples will look very different if the rock changes underneath. Look at the sketch map of Dundry Hill near Bristol (Fig c). Near the top of the hill the soil is thin and full of bits of limestone. Down the slope it is a clay soil because the rock beneath is a shale (clay) rock. Would you expect the soil on the lower slope to be a thick or thin layer? Give your reasons.

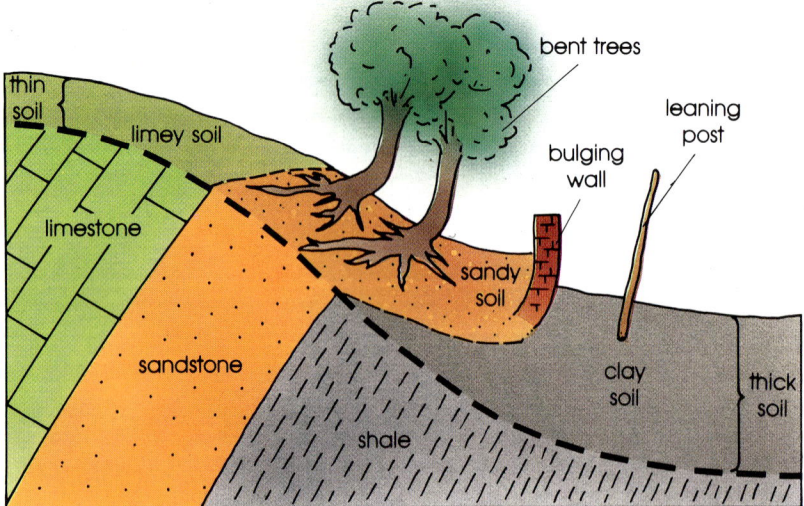

B Soil creep.

Activity 4.11

Comparing soils from different rocks

The soil samples you collected in Activity 4.10 will have come from many different places. Look carefully at each sample and record your findings in a table like this:

	Soil A	Soil B	Soil C	Soil D
Colour				
Feel – gritty or smooth				
Dampness				
Smell				
Amount of humus				
Other comments				

Activity 4.12

Comparing soil grains in different soils

1 Choose two *dry* soil samples which are different from each other, eg a sandy soil and a clay soil.

2 Break up any soil lumps in a mortar, using a pestle.

3 Fill a 200 ml measuring cylinder to the 100 ml mark. Then tip the ground-up soil into the measuring cylinder (Fig d). Watch carefully for several minutes to see what happens.

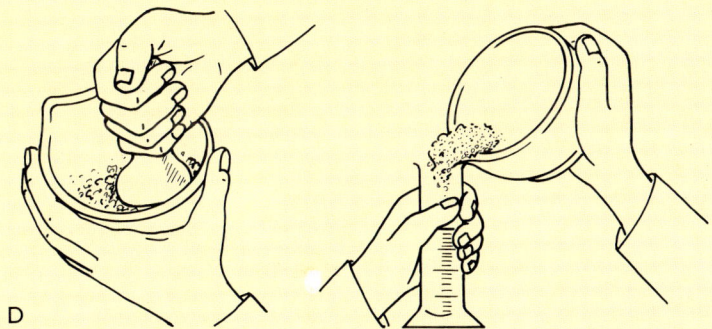

D

4 Note down what you see:

 a Does the soil settle into layers? Is the bottom layer **sand**? If so, why has it settled first?

 b Often a **silt** layer may form above the sand. Is this second layer a different colour?

 c The finest grains of all in soil are **clay**. It may take a day for this layer to settle out of the cloudy water.

5 Make sketches of each sample you test and show the difference in thickness of the layers. Label the layers.

6 Write about the differences between the soils you test.

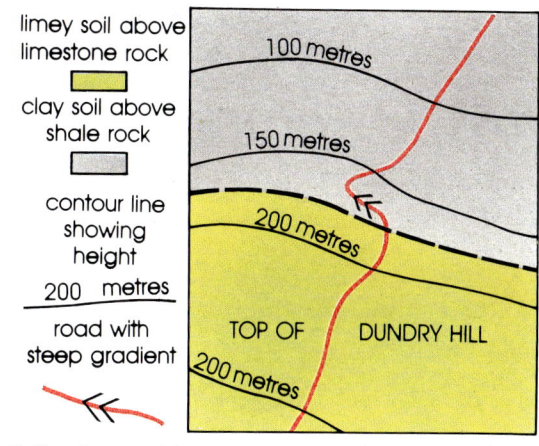

limey soil above limestone rock

clay soil above shale rock

contour line showing height

200 metres

road with steep gradient

TOP OF DUNDRY HILL

C Sketch map of Dundry Hill, Bristol. Where is the soil thickest?

Now try these

1 What kind of soil will come from these parent rocks: limestone, sandstone, shale?

2 In what order would you expect clay, silt and sand to settle out?

3 Complete the word puzzle (Fig e) using these clues:

 1 Soil slowly moves down this.

 2 Broken down rock.

 3 Used to find places.

 4 A tool for taking soil samples.

 5 Slow soil movement.

 6 Coarser soil grains.

 7 Slightly wet.

 8 This settles in water.

 9 Used to grind lumps.

 10 The rock a soil comes from.

E

EARTH IN SPACE

5.1 The Sun and the planets

Lotti, Liz and Tom were walking home one night. They looked up and could see stars and the Moon. 'I wonder how many stars there are up there,' said Tom.

'Did you know that each star is a sun, giving out its own light?' said Lotti.

'However many stars there are, they are not as big nor as bright as the Moon,' said Liz.

'The Moon only seems big because it is so close to the Earth,' said Lotti.

'What is the Moon, then?' asked Liz.

'It's really a planet that goes round the Earth,' said Tom. 'It has no light of its own. Moonlight is just sunlight shining off the Moon's surface.'

The Sun

The Sun is our nearest star. The temperature on its surface is 6000 degrees Celsius. The Sun is mostly made of hydrogen gas. It lets out huge amounts of energy as heat and sunlight. Enormous arches of glowing gases spurt out 500 000 kilometres from the Sun's surface (Fig a). The Sun radiates heat and light energy into space.

The solar system

The solar system is made up of the Sun together with the planets, comets and asteroids in orbit around it. The Sun is huge compared to the 'specks' of planets, comets and asteroids. Just a one-thousandth part of the Sun's mass would be equal to the mass of all the rest of the solar system. Fig b shows the distances from the Sun of the nine main planets. Notice that although the Earth is 150 million kilometres from the Sun, it is very close compared to the outer planets.

Planets are very different from stars. They have no light of their own. They can be seen because sunlight shines off them.

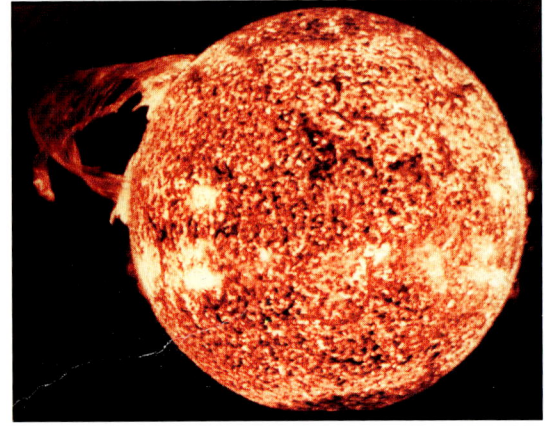

A The Sun with a jet of glowing gas called a prominence.

Activity 5.1

The scale of distances

Imagine that you are preparing for a space flight to the planets and you need to know how far each planet is from the Sun. The distance from the Sun to the Earth rounds off to 150 million kilometres. This Sun-Earth distance is called an **Astronomical Unit** (AU). If a spacecraft was to travel at 1000 km per hour (621 mph), it would take just over 17 years to cover the distance.

1 Complete a table like the one **CP** below. First, mark off the scale of AUs in Fig b onto a piece of scrap paper. Then put the scrap paper next to the line of planets. Read off the number of AUs from the Sun to each planet. Write in the distances on your table.

Planet	Distance in AUs

2 How many years would it take a spacecraft to reach Pluto travelling from Earth at 1000 km an hour?

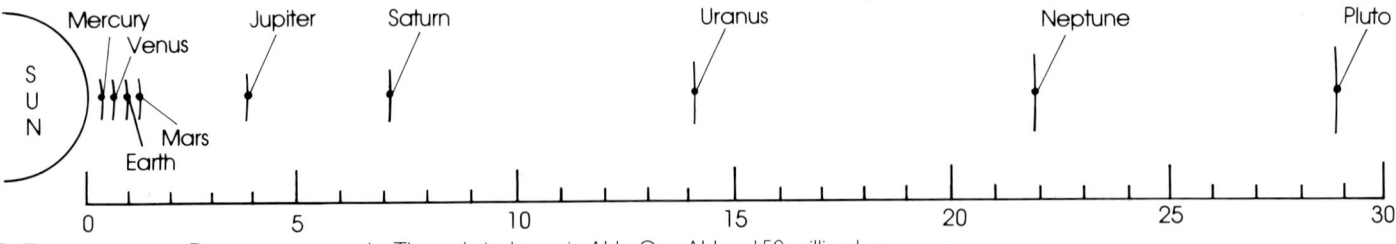

B The solar system. Distances are to scale. The scale is drawn in AUs. One AU = 150 million km.

Fortunately the unmanned space probes such as the American Voyager probes can travel much faster than 1000 km per hour. Even so, it took over 12 years for Voyager 2 to travel from Earth to Neptune. This probe is heading away from the solar system into outer space. Onboard is a record carrying details of 100 pictures of the Earth and spoken greetings. Fig c is a copy of the plaque sent into space by the Pioneer space probes. The hope is that one day some alien will find it and make contact.

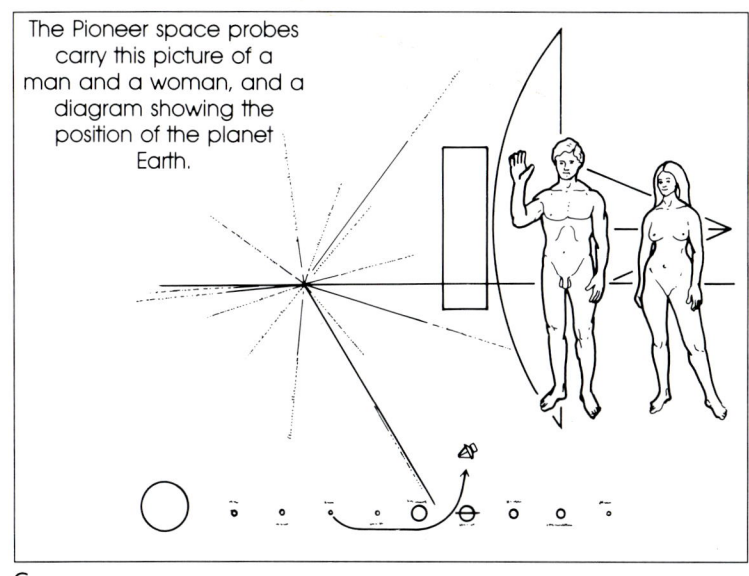

The Pioneer space probes carry this picture of a man and a woman, and a diagram showing the position of the planet Earth.

C

The planets

Fig d shows the size of the planets.

Mercury has a thin atmosphere and no water.

Venus is a very hot planet. It has a thick atmosphere of sulphuric acid.

Mars is about the same size as the core of the Earth. It is reddish in colour because of the sandstorms on its surface. It has an atmosphere and there is some water, mostly trapped in the polar ice caps. There are big volcanoes on Mars, and it has 2 moons.

Jupiter is a huge ball of hydrogen and helium. It has more than twice the mass of all the other planets put together. Swirling clouds cover the planet. Jupiter has 16 moons. One of them, called Io, is covered with volcanoes erupting molten sulphur.

Saturn has bright rings around it as well as 20 moons.

Uranus is a cold, rocky planet with a methane atmosphere. It is surrounded by faint rings and 15 moons.

Neptune has a rocky surface with water, liquid methane and ammonia, and has a thick atmosphere. It has rings and 8 moons.

Pluto is a tiny planet likely to be frozen methane with a thin atmosphere. It has one moon called Charon.

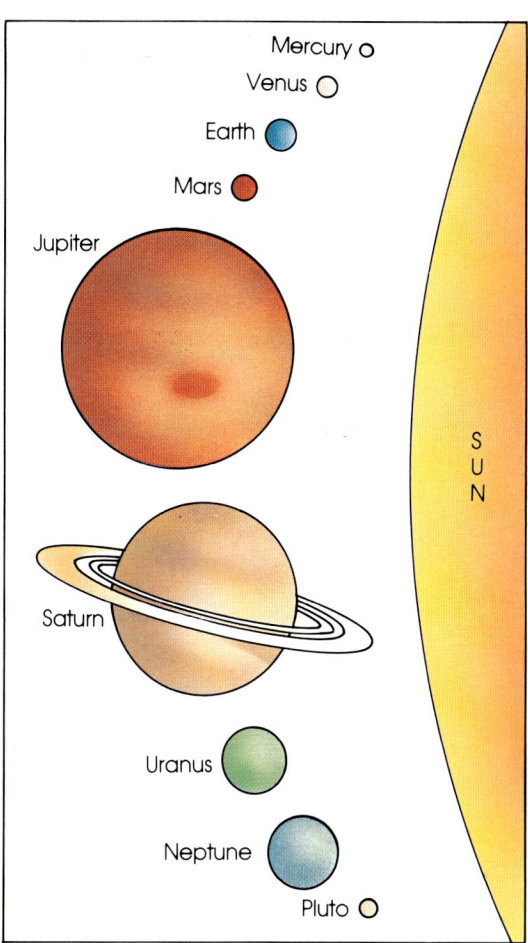

D The sizes of the planets, to scale.

Now try these

1 How is a planet different from a star?
2 How far is the Earth from the Sun?
3 What is the surface temperature of the Sun?
4 What is meant by a solar prominence?
5 Which is the solar system's biggest planet?
6 What are the names of the planet and its moon with volcanoes on it erupting sulphur?
7 Write about a 'Journey (WP) through the solar system'. Write about how long your journey takes and what you see at each planet on the way. Try to think of a better way of communicating with aliens — what would you take with you to tell them what Earth is like?

61

EARTH IN SPACE

5.2 How the Earth moves through space

Here are some questions Lotti, Liz and Tom asked about the Earth and the answers they found:

How does the Earth move?

The Earth moves through space in two different ways. It travels around the Sun in an oval path called an **orbit** (see Fig a). It is held in this position by the pull of the Sun's gravity. At the same time it turns on its axis, much like a spinning top.

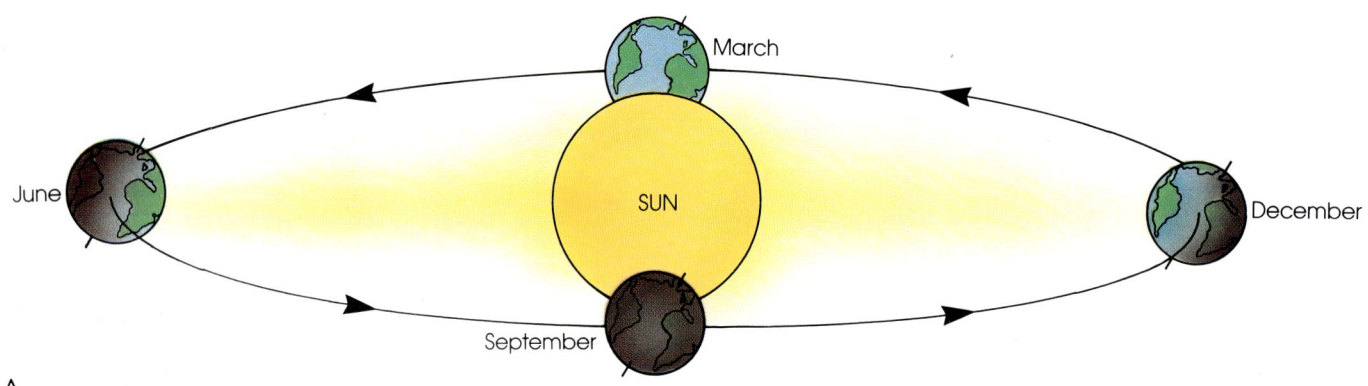

A

What is the Earth's axis?

The Earth's **axis** is an imaginary line which runs through the centre of the Earth from the North Pole to the South Pole.

Why are there days and years?

It takes the Earth 365 days and 6 hours to complete one orbit of the Sun. This is the length of one **year**. An extra day is added when there is a leap year to use up the extra 6 hours. It only takes 24 hours (one day) to complete one 'spin' on its own axis.

Why is there day and night?

You can see from Fig b that the Earth's axis is tilted slightly off the vertical. The angle of tilt is 23½ degrees. When one side of the Earth is in daylight, the other side is in darkness. Since one complete spin takes 24 hours, you might expect that night and day would be the same length everywhere on the Earth. However, for many places on the Earth the 24-hour day does not always divide equally into 12 hours of light and 12 hours of darkness. Instead, the length of daylight changes according to the time of year. In summer the daylight is longer and in winter the daylight is shorter.

Why are there seasons?

When the northern half, or **hemisphere**, of the Earth is tilted towards the Sun, it receives the Sun's direct rays. It is warmer and the days are longer – it is summer. At the same time, the southern hemisphere receives the weaker, slanting rays of the Sun, making it cooler with shorter days – it is winter.

When the southern hemisphere tilts towards the Sun, it receives the Sun's direct rays – this is the southern summer.

At the same time the northern hemisphere is tilted away from the Sun. This means it receives the weaker, slanting rays of the Sun. This is the northern winter.

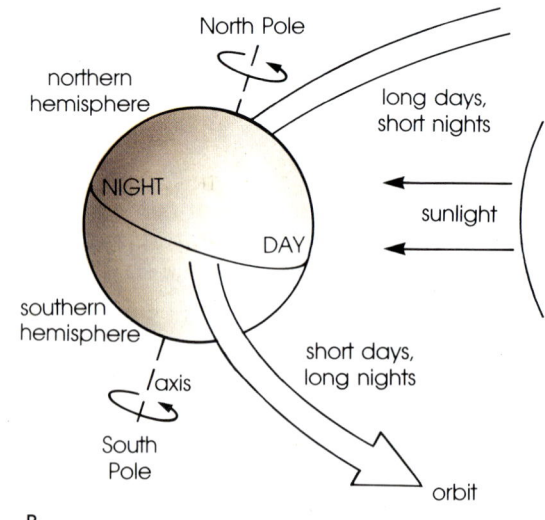

B

What is the equator?

This is an imaginary line around the Earth. It separates the two hemispheres. The equator is never tilted away from the Sun. The Sun's rays shine directly onto it, so it is always hot there. Places at or near to the equator do not have a winter and summer. The only changes in seasons are from dry to rainy conditions.

What is day and night like at the Poles?

The changing position of the Earth means that for a few weeks at the height of the northern summer, the North Pole has 24 hours of daylight. At the same time the South Pole has continuous night. The opposite is true in the southern summer.

Activity 5.2

Seasonal positions
1 What is the seasonal position of the Earth in Fig b? Is it 'northern summer/southern winter' or 'southern summer/northern winter'?
2 What is the seasonal position in Fig d?
3 What is the shortest day in the southern winter?
4 What is the longest day of the year in Australia?

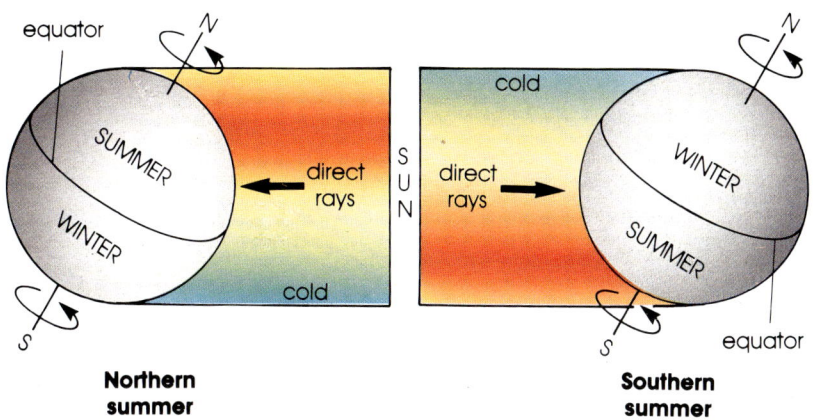

C

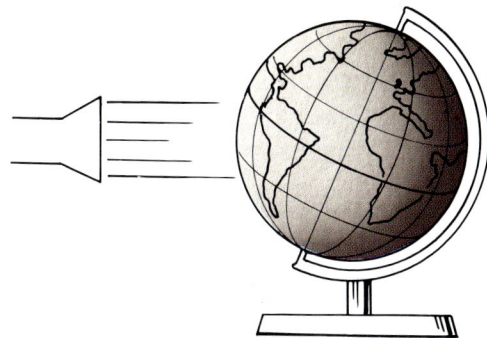

D Where light falls on the Earth.

Activity 5.3

The seasons
Darken the room. Use a torch to represent sunlight. Shine the torch at a globe of the Earth (Fig d). Notice how some parts of the globe get more light than other parts. Spin the globe and notice how the Earth turns through 'day' and 'night'. What happens at the North and South Poles of the globe?

Using Fig a as a guide, move the globe around the torch through the positions of the seasons. You should be able to see the effect of the tilt of the Earth's axis. Note how the Earth slopes *away* from the Sun in winter and *towards* the Sun in summer.

Look carefully at the positions of the Earth in autumn and spring. These are the 'in-between' seasons when the northern and southern hemispheres receive equal amounts of sunshine. What is the day length in these positions? It is a good idea to make labelled sketches to show each season.

Now try these

1 What is the Earth's axis?
2 How many times does the Earth spin on its axis whilst making one orbit of the Sun?
3 How long is one complete day?
4 Explain why the daylight hours are longer in summer and shorter in winter.
5 Where would you have to go to sunbathe at midnight **a** in June, **b** in December?

GLOSSARY

Anemometer An instrument to measure wind speed.
Anticline An upfold in rock layers.
Ash Powdered rock produced by volcanic explosions.
Astronomical Unit One unit is the average distance from the Earth to the Sun, 150 million kilometres.
Atoll An island in tropical seas made entirely of coral.
Axis An imaginary line which runs through the centre of the Earth, around which the Earth rotates.

Bathylith An igneous intrusion where magma has cooled slowly underground.
Bomb A lump of molten lava thrown out of a volcano in an eruption.

Celsius Temperature scale where water freezes at 0°C and boils at 100°C.
Cementation The process by which grains of rock are stuck together.
Compaction The settling and pressing together of rock grains in sediments.
Condensation Moisture droplets produced by rapid cooling of damp air.
Conglomerate A sedimentary rock made of pebbles cemented together.
Crater The depression found at the summit of a volcano.

Earthquake The shaking of the Earth caused by sudden rock movements.
Epicentre The nearest point at the surface to the focus of an earthquake.
Equator An imaginary line at right angles to the axis through the poles, dividing the two hemispheres (halves) of the Earth's sphere.
Erosion The wearing away of the land surface by water, ice, wind and movements caused by gravity.
Eruption A sudden escape of gases, ash and lava from a volcano.
Evaporation The change from a liquid to a gas caused by heating and air movements.

Focus Underground location of a rock movement that causes an earthquake.
Fossil The preserved remains of an animal or plant, found in rocks.

Glacier A slowly moving river of ice.

Hemisphere Half of the Earth's sphere, as divided by the equator.
Humidity The amount of moisture in the air.
Humus Rotted plant and animal material found in soil.

Igneous A type of rock formed from cooling of molten magma or lava.

Lava Molten magma that erupts at the surface.
Limestone A sedimentary rock made of calcium carbonate.

Magma Molten rock which exists in pockets below ground.
Metamorphic Any rock changed by heat and/or pressure.

Nutrients Plant foods found in soil.

Orbit The path of movement of one heavenly body around another in space.
Ore A mineral deposit containing metals that are worthwhile to extract.

Pipe The central channel in a volcano conducting material to the surface.
Pumice An aerated, frothy lava.

Rain gauge An instrument that records the amount of rainfall.

Sandstone A sedimentary deposit of sand.
Sediment A deposit of loose material produced by erosion of the land and carried by water until it settles as the current slows.
Sedimentary Rocks produced by the settling of sediments.
Seismometer An instrument used to record earthquake shock waves.
Shale A sedimentary deposit of mud.
Soil creep The slow movement of soil and loose rock down a slope.
Stalactite Icicle-like structure formed by the deposition of calcium carbonate (lime) in limestone caves.
Stalagmite A pillar-like structure found beneath stalactites in limestone caves, formed by deposition of lime from the dripping water.
Static electricity The build up of an electric charge in an object, or in a cloud by the uprush of air.
Syncline A downfold in rock layers.

Thermometer An instrument used to record temperature.
Tsunami A large, destructive sea wave produced by earthquakes or volcanoes.

Vent The hole through which erupted material leaves a volcano.
Volcano A cone-shaped mountain formed by the eruption of lava and ash deposited around its vent.

Water cycle The circulation of water through the atmosphere and the Earth's surface.
Weathering The breakdown of rocks by exposure to the weather.
Wind vane An instrument used to record wind direction.